Room to Grow

Making Your Child's Bedroom An Exciting World

Sharon Owen Haven
Illustrated by
Myland McRevey

Two Step Books
Berkeley, California

Copyright © 1979 by Sharon Owen Haven
All rights reserved.
Library of Congress Cataloging in Publication Data

Haven, Sharon Owen, 1943-
    Room to grow.

    1. Children's rooms. 2. Interior decoration.
I. Title.
NK2117.C4H38   747'.76   79-15257
ISBN 0-931018-02-1

Published by
Two Step Books, 2490 Channing Way #210, Berkeley, CA 94704

For my children Matthew and Amy, my inspiration, and their father, Clayton, who picks up his saw and hammer and gives my inspiration substance.

Contents

Illustrations

Acknowledgements

This book began at the suggestion of Liza Cohen. Thanks to her professional competence, invaluable advice, and her unflagging support and enthusiasm, it has become a reality. But most important, she has made the endeavor a delightful and gratifying experience.

1
Asking the
Basic Questions

A child's bedroom is more than a place to sleep. It's a child's retreat, laboratory, stage and palette. Because it must accommodate a variety of activities, a child's room presents a special challenge to parent and designer alike. Designing a child's room raises unique considerations of scale, safety, and age-related interests which are unlike those of any other room in the house. But, beyond all the practical considerations, a child's room is a world of its own. You can make this world a wonderful and exciting place.

Room to Grow provides a framework so that you can approach the practical aspects of creating your child's room one step at a time. It includes a myriad of ideas to help stimulate your creative thinking. The ideas in this book are easy and inexpensive.

While some of the issues and ideas discussed here will be relevant to teenagers, the book is primarily intended for the rooms of children under age thirteen. By the time a child reaches the teenage years, his needs and interests are more adult. He frequently has his own very firm ideas regarding the design of his room. (Please excuse the conventional use of the universal masculine pronoun throughout the book. It is for convenience and readability and does not reflect any sexist bias of the author.)

Room to Grow is also a workbook. The illustrations were designed to be colored in. The questionnaire was designed to be filled out. The page size was chosen to accommodate your own ideas and additions. Most of all, this book is for you to use. Have fun with it!

A child's room must serve many people's needs and interests, so it is well worth the time to sit down and ask yourself and your child a few basic questions about what you both want from this room. If you establish your needs and priorities *first*, you can avoid expensive or inconvenient mistakes. The chances of everyone being satisfied with the results are greater. Following are some basic questions to ask yourself:

How many children are going to use this room and what are their ages and sex? Children have different requirements in terms of interests, scale, color, and safety as they grow older. Does the sex of your child affect your ideas about room design? It might be useful for you to examine your feelings or assumptions about this issue before you start. You might be enthralled with the idea of a frilly canopied bed for your daughter's room, while her major concern is where she is going to house her snakes.

If this room is shared, you have to consider additional needs like privacy and whether you view this arrangement as temporary or permanent. These factors will affect some of the choices you make concerning space-sharing. Ask your children their feelings about sharing a room. Are they enthusiastic about being together? Do they have intense needs for privacy? Most children have some need for privacy. If you do not provide it, they may divide up their space in less successful ways. Space-sharing ideas are discussed in detail in a later section, but it is important to be aware of your children's attitudes from the beginning.

Are there any health problems to be considered? Allergic children may require special kinds of hypo-allergenic flooring, bedding, and curtains. Handicapped children have specialized requirements for their rooms. But even the child who tends to catch colds can be aided by a room arrangement that minimizes drafts.

Who is going to be primarily responsible for maintenance? If the child maintains the room, plan the room so it will be easy for the child to clean it up himself. If you take care of the room, perhaps your major interest will be in a "labor saving" plan. By agreeing on a maintenance scheme and standard to which everyone can commit themselves first, and then planning a room which facilitates the scheme, you avoid some of those "household battles" about tidiness.

Should controlling noise be given a high priority in planning your child's room? This will depend largely on the physical lay-out of your home and your personal tolerance for noise. If your two young sons share a room directly above your study, controlling noise may be a major concern. If, on the other hand, their room is at the opposite end of the house, it might not be a problem at all.

How long do you want your child's room to last? A significant number of decisions you make in planning your child's room will depend on how long you want it to last, and how long you plan to be in your home. You may not opt for "built-ins" if you intend to sell your home in a year. There will be more limitations designing a room in a rented home than in your own.

It is possible to design a room whose major components will last through childhood if the room is made sufficiently flexible and adjustable. On the other hand, you and your child might want to start all over from time to time.

Since our culture is extremely mobile (changing homes on an average of every seven years), a later section will be devoted to ideas for people who rent or move frequently.

What activities will take place in this room? Try listing all the activities that you anticipate or that your child would like to take place in this room. Interests change radically from age to age, and it is easier to design a room to accommodate new activities than it is to re-do the room entirely every time your child has a new all-consuming interest. Here is a list of activities that may take place within the four walls of a child's room:

Sleeping	Watching television
Reading	Playing with clay/playdough
Painting/drawing	Cutting and pasting
Dancing	Caring for pets
Playing/listening to music	Making a puppet theater
Studying	Entertaining friends
Dressing up	Climbing and jumping
Playing with toys, puzzles, games, dolls	Doing hobbies
	Acting

You can undoubtedly think of many more. Every child and family has varying needs. You may live in an urban apartment house in an area that has inclement weather. Your child's room may have to accommodate just about everything including vigorous activity. On the other hand, if you live in an area where outdoor activity is accessible, or you have a playroom (or recreational area), your child's room may not have to be the central location of all his activities.

What are your child's favorite colors? While you are exploring your child's preferences, ask him about color. (See the section on color in Chapter 2.) If your child is pre-verbal, watch his play and see what colored toys he seems to enjoy the most. Offer him the same toy in different colors and see which he chooses. A child has color preferences at an early age and though the preferences may change through time, they are extremely important.

How much money do you want to spend? When you know your monetary limits, begin assessing what is feasible for your child's room. For example, you might want to make your major investment a durable bed and chest of drawers and spend less money on the remaining components which are easier to change. Obviously, you'll want to avoid running out of money half-way through the project with some of the necessities left unprovided. A successful design does not depend on a large investment. You may already have furniture for the room and want a design which accommodates it. In this case, your investment might be a can of paint, a few inexpensive accessories, and a little bit of elbow grease. The more you are able to make or provide yourself, the less the room will cost. There are numerous inexpensive or do-it-yourself alternatives discussed in the following pages.

Are there any conflicts between what you and your child want? Try asking your child: what do you want from your room? Or, what do you want your room to be to you? Then, ask yourself the same question. The answers to this basic question can provide the foundation for whatever the room becomes. Your child might answer: "I want this room to be my special place where I can do anything I want." And you might answer: "I want this room to be a stimulating place where my child will want to spend much of his time without requiring my involvement." These answers turn out to be complimentary and your goal then becomes designing a room which reflects the child's interests. On the other hand, if you find that what you want from this room conflicts in some respects, you need to find a solution that will satisfy both of you.

If your child is pre-verbal, you will have to observe his activities, interests, and personality to assess what his needs are. Try taking an hour to do nothing but watch his behavior at play. What kinds of activities does he prefer at this stage? How does he approach different situations? Is he cautious or adventurous? What kind of stimulation does he respond to most? All of these answers will give you clues about how to design his room most effectively. If your child is an infant, turn to the section on the nursery. (This "stage" is given special consideration because it is so brief and infants have similar needs.)

There may be other considerations particular to your child or your situation which have not been mentioned. If they are important to you, be sure to consider them in your planning. Your child's room will not satisfy him or you if it does not meet both your needs, so the first step is to articulate and understand what they are. The following questionnaire offers a handy means of keeping these needs and priorities in front of you as you choose the individual elements of your child's room.

BASIC QUESTIONS

Numbers How many children will live
in this room? _____

Is this a temporary or
permanent arrangement? _____

If the room is to be shared, should
privacy needs be given priority? _____

Age _____

Sex _____

Health Are there any health problems
which need to be considered? _____

Maintenance Who is primarily responsible for
maintenance of child's room? _____

Is a low maintenance design to be
given high priority? _____

Noise Is controlling noise to be given
a high priority? _____

Duration Do you rent or own your home? _____

How long do you plan on living
in your present home? _____

How long do you want this plan for
your child's room to last? _____

Activities What activities are going to take
place in this room? _____

Color What are the child's favorite
colors? _____

Budget How much do you want to spend
on this room? _____

**Needs
Summary** What does the child want from
this room? _____

What does the parent want from
this room? _____

Do these in any way conflict? _____

Any Other Considerations

6

2
The Elements
of a Child's Room

Once you've figured out what your priorities are, you can explore the possibilities that are open to you. Remember to take elements like scale, age, and safety into account. Consider them first because they are of primary importance and will influence the other decisions you make about your child's room.

Scale

Homes are designed, built, and furnished for adults. Have you ever gotten down on your hands and knees and taken a child-sized tour of your home? You may find that *everything* appears huge and hard to reach; the major part of your visual landscape is the "underside" of things. You may not be able to avoid this perspective in most of the home, but a child's room should be his size.

Quite naturally, children feel most comfortable in surroundings scaled to their size. It can be terribly frustrating to sit at a table that is too high, or on a chair that does not allow your feet to touch the floor, or to crane your neck to see a favorite picture, or to be unable to reach a special toy because the shelf is too high. When a child is frustrated, he may give up.

Furniture and equipment that are too big tempt children to climb, often precariously, to reach for items that are too high. The child and the desired toy may both fall.

If your child's room is out of scale, it will cause you a great deal of inconvenience. If a child cannot reach his toys, or get his clothes out of high drawers, or reach the closet hangers, then *you* are going to have to do it. And you are also going to put these things away! If you want your child to take care of dressing himself, putting his toys away, and keeping his room orderly, then you should create a room that is at his level. If you give high priority to planning a room that your child will maintain, you must pay careful attention to scale.

The following two charts list the most commonly used measurements in standing and sitting positions from age two to thirteen. Please keep in mind that the figures are averages. Since your child may vary greatly from the averages, you may want to keep your scale as flexible as possible. The charts do furnish you with an approximate idea of scale for your child's room. It is unlikely that you will adjust your child's furniture every year, but you may want to choose a median scale that will last a few years. These charts also give you a sense of how long your existing scale will last until it is outgrown.

Reach

Height

Eye Level

Age	Eye Level	Height	Reach
2	33*	36	43
3	36	39	46
4	38	42	50
5	40	45	53
6	41	46	56
7	44	48	59
8	46	51	63
9	49	53	65
10	51	55	68
11	53	58	72
12	55	60	74
13	57	62	77

*Averaged, in inches

1. Standing chart.

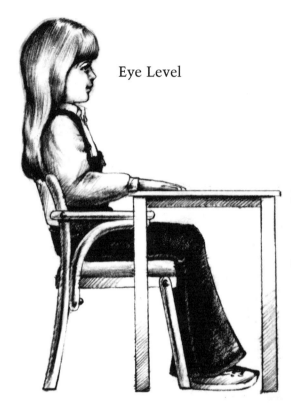

Eye Level

Desk Height

Chair Height

Age	Eye Level	Desk Height	Chair Height
2	25*	14	7
3	27	15	8
4	29	16	10
5	31	17	11
6	32	18	12
7	34	19	12
8	35	20	13
9	37	21	14
10	38	22	14
11	40	23	15
12	41	23	15
13	43	24	16

*Averaged, in inches

2. *Sitting chart.*

Age

As mentioned earlier, children's requirements for their rooms vary greatly from age to age. Watch him. Your child's current interests will supply the best cues. There are, however, very broad developmental stages which children pass through. It is useful to be aware of what these general stages imply and how they might affect your design.

Birth to crawling (6-10 months). An infant's needs for his room are few and relate almost entirely to physical comfort and well-being. (See section on nursery in Chapter 3.)

Crawling to age 3. Once a child becomes mobile, his requirements change radically. This period is the age of exploration. It is also the most dangerous time in a child's life. At this stage your child needs a stimulating environment which encourages exploration and experimentation but which is, above all, safe! A child's own place offers him a great sense of security and stability amidst the rapid change and growth going on within.

Age 3-8. Children spend a large amount of time in their rooms during this period, and their rooms are very important to them. The most critical consideration during this period should be space to play. A room design which maximizes play area is most successful.

Age 8-13. In this period, children are growing up. Their activities and interests become more adult. They need study areas as well as play areas. As they approach age thirteen, their major interests shift toward music, reading, homework, and being with friends. It's useful to have a flexible room at this stage as interests and hobbies change.

Safety

Generally, the younger your child, the more important safety becomes in designing his room. The period between crawling and approximately age three, when a child discovers the world outside him and begins to explore it, is the most dangerous. Child development experts stress the importance of this period for later achievement. A dull, non-stimulating environment impairs curiosity, learning, creativity, and independence. On the other hand, your child needs protection. Children most commonly get burned, poisoned, stuck in small places, and fall during this period.

As a parent you are challenged to create an environment that is safe enough so that your child is reasonably free to experiment and explore as he likes. This task is not as difficult as it sounds. Once again try getting down on the floor and taking a child's eye view of his room (and your entire home) looking for potential safety hazards. Give all possible purchases a safety inspection. Before you do anything with your child's room, ask yourself if it is safe. Then make periodic safety inspections of both his room and your entire home, and ask yourself if it is *still* safe. Do not assume your child is too young or too small to get into a danger spot. Children learn quickly. What was safe last month may not be safe today.

Here is a list of safety ideas to keep in mind when you are designing your child's room:

- Make things easy to reach safely.

- Avoid Fiberglas fabrics. (Particles of glass can be inhaled.)

- Install a smoke alarm.

- Put safety locks on necessary cabinets and doors.

- Use only non-toxic paint.

- Avoid furniture that a child can pull over, or bolt those pieces to the wall or floor.

- Buy window guards if needed.

- Secure stairways. Use gates and cover rails if necessary.

- Avoid floor or desk lamps which can be overturned easily.

- Secure area rugs with double-sided tape so they will not slip.

- Before you invest in carpeting, investigate its response to fire. Some flame retardant carpeting emits dangerous gases when overheated.

- Check furniture for splinters or protruding nails.

Color

Never underestimate the power of color. It is probably the easiest, cheapest, and most important element you can supply in your child's room. You can use it to delight, excite, and stimulate your child's imagination. Color can also be used to soothe and relax your child.

Here's a summary of color relationships and terminology. Pick up your crayons, pens, or paints and color away!

Although designers have proved that there are no rigid "rules" regarding the successful use of color, it's helpful to know the general ways that color relationships affect a room. Some of the most important are:

- The larger the area covered by a color, the more it dominates.

- Too many colors can make a room busy and distracting. Too few can be dull and uninteresting.

- Since opposite colors lose their effect when used in equal proportions, it is usually more interesting to let one dominate.

- Light neutrals expand space. White makes a room appear its largest and raises the ceiling. Dark colors diminish space and lower a high ceiling.

- White increases the power of a nearby color.

- Color temperatures and values establish mood. Light and dull cool colors are the most quiet and subdued. Bright and dark warm colors are the most bold and spirited.

Child development experts have found that even newborn infants respond to color. It is more important than form in the early stages of a child's development. Although we know that mood is affected by color, a recent study claims that I.Q. can be related to color as well. In any case, a child will be happier in a room with colors he likes. As surprising as it seems, a child does have preferences, and he can communicate them as early as one year of age.

Let your child pick out the colors of his own room if possible. If he is too young to tell you his favorite colors, watch his play. Which crayons does he use most often? What colors generally dominate his art work? Color preferences among children will vary, but almost all children, and especially young children, are attracted to bright, true, primary colors over pastels. While there is no unanimity among children about favorite colors, there is nearly unanimous agreement about color *value.* Make it bright and bold.

Letting your child choose the colors for his room does not mean you are doomed to an eternity of orange and black. A child's color preferences at any particular point in time may be very strong, but they also may be short-lived. Favorite colors change with age. Since color is the fastest and least expensive way to change a room, you may want to indulge in periodic total color changes. Conversely, there are ways to maximize color flexibilty in your child's room so that you rarely have to paint or re-paper.

If you paint your child's room white, you'll have lots of flexibility when it comes to adding color. White brightens and sharpens other colors, and adds crispness and light. It is also available in satin finish enamels for easy care. You can then use your child's currently favorite colors in accessories like throw pillows, waste paper baskets, patterned sheets, area rugs, and inexpensive cotton curtains. All of these items can be changed easily. You can paint graphics or a picture on a wall. You can make the walls into display surfaces for your child's art. This solution gives your child the freedom to experiment with color. It also minimizes the redecorating burden for you. Color can be anywhere! Toys, rugs, art, curtains, bedding, and furniture are all good ways to make your child's room colorful.

You have a lot of freedom when it comes to color. Gone are the days when a child's room meant pastel monotones. Try using the rooms illustrated in the book to experiment with color. Don't be timid. When your child tells you his favorite color is blue, it probably isn't powder blue. You can be bold and playful with color in your child's room, so enjoy yourself. Your child will be delighted.

3. Teddy bear color chart. These are the six basic colors of the color circle. All colors consist of these colors or their combinations.

3A. *These are complementary colors—colors found directly opposite each other on the color circle. They emphasize each other when you put them next to each other. They are more vivid when seen together.*

3B. *These are analogous colors. They are neighbors on the color circle and are compatible when put together. They blend instead of creating sharp contrasts.*

4. *These are neutrals. They do not appear in the color circle, but can play important roles in your total color scheme.*

4A. Colors have temperatures. Some are warm and some are cool. They effect the "mood" of your room.

4B. Colors have a variety of values as well, from light to dark and dull to bright. These values determine color intensity.

Flooring

The floor is the most used surface in your child's room. For the first years it defines a child's world. He spends most of his waking time on the floor: he may even use it as his "table." After the pre-school years, children spend a great deal of time on the floor in a variety of activities—playing games, building blocks, riding toys, racing cars, or on their bellies, in fantasy play, etc. Choose your child's flooring with care. In addition to his activity needs, you will want to think about maintenance, durability, and expense.

There are basically three alternatives—wall-to-wall carpeting, hard smooth flooring (wood or linoleum), or a combination of hard floor and area rugs. They all have advantages and disadvantages.

Wall-to-wall carpeting has two major advantages. It absorbs noise, and it is soft. However, carpeting is hard to keep clean in a child's room, limits activities, and costs quite a bit to install.

Consider for a moment the variety of spills wall-to-wall carpeting will endure in a child's early years. There is milk, food, saliva, and the inevitable toilet-training accidents in the beginning, and then on to clay, pens, paints, glue, dirt, and sand. Chances are that you will either end up with an unsanitary and unsightly mess underfoot, or you will find yourself devoting a great deal of time and energy to cleaning up and preventing potentially messy activities.

Wall-to-wall carpeting limits activities. Since it is difficult to run trucks, cars, and trains on most carpeting, toys with wheels are likely to end up under your feet in the kitchen. Blocks fall over, and it is frustrating to try to ride toys on carpeting.

Given these disadvantages, you may not want to install wall-to-wall carpeting in a child's room. On the other hand, you may be renting a place that is carpeted or move into a home with new carpeting. In these cases, buy a large drop cloth for messy projects. If, in the end, you decide to buy wall-to-wall carpeting for your child's room, dark colors and tweeds are the most practical. (Don't forget to check all carpeting for its response to fire before you buy.) Reed, grass, or jute matting is not recommended because it has exaggerated cleaning problems and limited durability. It is hard on the knees and prevents a great number of activities.

A hard smooth floor, either wood or a variation of linoleum, is an alternative to wall-to-wall carpeting. A linoleum-type floor can be as expensive to install as carpeting, but has the advantages of lifetime durability, easy maintenance and maximum freedom of activity. A wooden floor, sanded for splinter-free safety and then painted, stained, or left natural and sealed with several coats of polyurethane, has all the advantages of a linoleum floor, often for a fraction of the cost. Of course, both wood or linoleum-type floors are hard, sometimes cold, and can exacerbate noise problems.

A combination of area rugs on a wood or linoleum-type floor allows you to enjoy the advantages of both carpeting and a hard floor. One or more thick, soft, *washable* rugs supply warmth and comfort to crawlers, and they help dampen noise. Area rugs can delineate different activity areas in a room. When they get dirty, they can be tossed into the washing machine. If they cover needed play space, you can push them aside or roll them up to provide a smooth surface. If you generally like wall-to-wall carpeting, you may opt for one large rug which covers a great portion of the room. You can still roll up this large rug when you need space for various activities. Of course, the larger the rug, the more awkward the cleaning.

If you want to get the maximum use out of your child's floor, make it *more* than a floor. A couple of varieties of commercial carpeting for children's rooms have games printed on them. Here are some other ideas:

- Use strippable, pressure-sensitive vinyl coated paper to cut out games, pictures, roads, etc. These can be pressed on the floor, then removed and discarded when they are no longer wanted.

- Paint pathways, a giant maze, or graphics on the floor.

- Paint an over-sized game on your child's floor: monopoly, checkers, hopscotch, etc.

- Use your floor as a learning tool by painting or cutting numbers, colors, or your child's name out of carpet remnants.

- Make a giant game board out of carpet remnants.

- Make your child's floor into an ocean by adding pillows in the shape of undersea creatures.

You can probably think of many more; your child can suggest other ideas too! While practical concerns tend to dominate decisions about flooring, it is important to remember that the floor of a child's room can be an innovative and fun place.

Walls and Ceilings

The walls and ceilings contain the largest amount of surface space in your child's room. Some of this space will be diminished by furniture like beds, dressers, bookshelves, storage units, or desks. The rest (along with the floor, if you choose) is your canvas. You and your child can do an infinite number of wonderful things with this canvas. Just keep in mind that it is much to your advantage to make these surfaces *washable*.

The walls (and sometimes ceilings) get more abuse in a child's room than in other rooms. Here are the merits of different wall coverings:

Paint. It is cheap, simple to apply, and available in every color imaginable. You can buy satin finish enamels which are non-toxic and easy to clean. Paint is also the least complicated wall covering to change. When it starts to show signs of wear and tear, or your child is tired of the color, paint over the old coat.

Wallpaper. Although this wall covering has less flexibility than paint, many parents find it appealing. The problems with wallpaper are: it can be difficult to apply and expensive. If your child tires of the pattern, it is not as easy to change as paint. Unless it is vinyl-coated, it is not washable. Vinyl wallpapers are easy to clean and available in either plain or patterned variations, but they are difficult to paint over and cannot be papered over. You can paint over paperbacked burlap but it has the other disadvantages of wallpaper, and it fades quickly. Perhaps the greatest disadvantage of wallpaper is that a loose corner can provide an irresistible temptation to a child.

Paneling. This category includes standard vertical wood paneling, shingles, and cedar strips. These wall covers are quite durable but generally involve a major investment. They are time-consuming to install and hard to change, so they should be viewed as permanent. Maintenance depends largely on how they are finished. A washable sealer or finish coat of polyurethane is the most practical kind of finish. Unless they are painted, these varieties of paneling will provide a natural wood surface which often adds a dark, heavy appearance to a child's room. If you like paneling, you may want to restrict it to one wall.

Pegboard. You may not want to cover your child's entire room with pegboard, but it is useful in limited areas. With hooks or shelves added and enamel-painted a bright color, it attractively displays a child's hobby, treasures, or craft tools. It is relatively inexpensive, durable, easy to install, and washable if painted with enamels. You can paint over it, remove it, or simply move the hooks and shelves around. It provides flexibility for children whose hobbies or interests change frequently.

Bulletin board surfaces. This type of wall-covering falls into two categories: fiberboard (Homasote or Upson) and cork. Fiberboard is inexpensive, easy to put up, and can be painted or covered with burlap, canvas, or fabric. It will last unless you mount a dart board on it or subject it to special abuse. Cork may be more attractive but it has less adaptability. It costs more and tends to crumble. Because it cannot be painted very successfully, you are limited to a very dark surface. High quality cork lasts for a long time but costs more; you may choose to use it in small areas.

Fabric. You can also cover your child's walls with fabric, which is available in a wide price range. Sometimes a fanciful king-sized bed sheet will cover an entire wall for a reasonable amount. You can apply fabric by rolling or brushing liquid starch onto the wall and then putting the smooth fabric on top. You can remove the fabric at any time without damaging the walls. This is a good way to camouflage damaged or uneven walls. You can also attach fabric to the wall with Velcro (a hook and loop fastener—one strip glued to the wall, the other sewn on the sheet). When the sheet is dirty, simply pull it down and throw it in the washing machine. Of course, if you shirr (gather at top and bottom) your fabric, you will need to buy more fabric. Even with a limited budget, you can create something magical in your child's room with fabric and a little imagination.

You have a wide range of materials to choose from when it comes to wall coverings. You can also combine these wall coverings in an endless number of ways.

Design alternatives for walls in a child's rooms are as varied as a child's imagination. With paint alone you can:

- Paint one wall or all the walls the same color or different colors and add a dado above or below (a dado is a decorative strip which divides the lower wall from the upper wall.)

- Paint the room white and make it a gallery for your child's art and collections.

- Paint a mural or a picture or a supergraphic on the walls.

- Use stencils and paint designs around a wall or a dado.

- Buy blackboard paint and make one wall a giant blackboard.

- Paint your child's name in giant letters on a wall or walls.

Ceilings should not be neglected either. Just remember that a dark ceiling appears lower and more confining; a light ceiling appears higher. Anything you can do with a wall, you can also do with a ceiling. In addition, you can add real or stick-on beams or cover it with acoustical tile for noise absorption. Ceilings are special because you can *hang* things from them. Using ceilings this way often frees up valuable floor space for other purposes. It also produces some delightful effects in a child's room. Here are a few ways to use your ceiling as a hanging surface:

- Suspend lamps. Hanging lamps cannot be knocked over.

- Hang a group of storage baskets.

- Run a climbing pole from floor to ceiling.

- Hang plants.

- Suspend mobiles, kites, birds, airplanes, balloons, toys, etc.

- Hang the bed and/or chairs for a different effect. It makes floor care easier.

- Paint the ceiling blue and hang fluffy, stuffed pillow clouds.

If you use your ceiling as a hanging surface, be absolutely certain that the objects are *securely* anchored. A serious accident could occur if a heavy object were to fall on your child. Screw sturdy hooks into wood-only beams, joists, etc. Toggle bolts will support some items in a drywall or plaster ceiling. Check your ceiling first and get informed advice if necessary. Your ceiling may need alteration if you want to use it as a hanging surface.

The floors, walls, and ceiling define your child's room and set its limits. Try viewing them altogether as a large canvas. Ask your child to sit at the entrance of his room and imagine it as a big picture. What does he see? If you and your child are uninspired or overwhelmed by the alernatives, look at magazines, friend's rooms, pictures or books for some ideas. A successful room must reflect your child's interests and taste. The chances are you will never find such a room, but will have to create it yourself. The following illustrations, however, show a few of the possible directions you might take.

5. *Dado—hooks and bulletin board. This is one way to make use of a dado which divides the wall into upper and lower spaces. The upper wall is covered with inexpensive fiberboard and painted. It becomes a giant bulletin board which can display a child's art, favorite pictures, calendar, clock, chalkboard, and other mementos. Hooks screwed into the dado provide convenient places to hang clothes and toys. You may want to try this idea on a regular wall by adding a narrow strip of wood across the length of it.*

6. *Name on Wall—Jenny. The occupant of this room will never be in question. Children love to see their names. This is an easy and inexpensive way to personalize a wall of your child's room.*

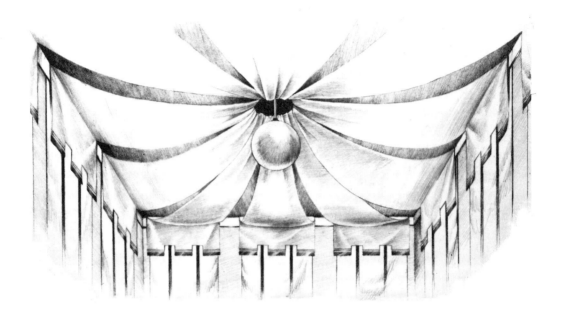

7. *Covering walls with fabric is one way to give a child's room color and charm and cover up damaged or ugly walls at the same time. Here, striped sheets are attached to the wall with Velcro or staples. Ceiling panels of fabric are gathered on a ring centered around a ceiling light fixture. They are then stretched outwards to the ceiling. If you use inexpensive fabric, this can be a reasonable and easy way to transform your child's walls. A Velcro fastener will enable you to remove the fabric for laundering without great effort.*

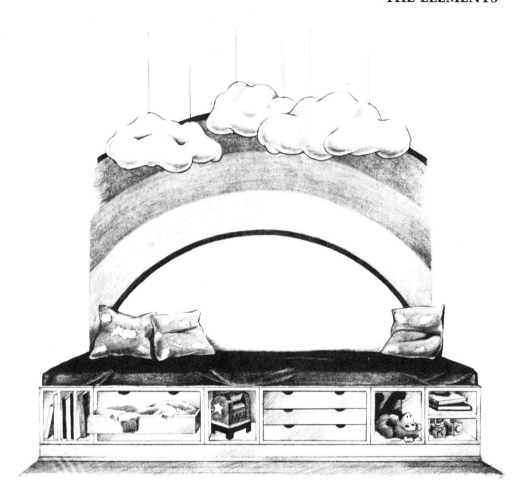

8. Bright bands of color create a rainbow on the wall. Storage modules with a pad on top double as seating. Clouds are fluffy stuffed pillows which hang from the ceiling.

9. Graphics are another way to give your child's walls drama and personality. Graphic kits are available commercially, but this one is simple to do yourself. Here the graphic is incorporated into a corner play platform and pit.

10. This room makes maximum use of its ceiling surface with a hanging bed, chair, lamp, tropical bird, climbing pole and plant. Notice how use of the ceiling frees floor space. A jungle mural on the wall transforms this end of the room into an exotic setting for fun and fantasy play. You can easily create a wall mural by projecting a slide photograph of the scene you want onto the wall and tracing along the lines.

Windows and Doors

Windows often become the focal point of a room because they are the source of natural light. Remember that children use their rooms during daylight hours. Sunlight is always preferable to artificial light for a child's activities, so whatever treatment you give your child's windows, do not diminish their light-providing properties.

You may ask yourself if you need a window covering at all, especially if your child's window affords an attractive view and privacy. If your child naps during the day, you may want a way to darken the room for that period. There are numerous ways to accomplish this without sacrificing a window's light-providing capacity. Window coverings are used to control light but some are more flexible than others. This list suggests the variety of window coverings available to you:

Shades. With window shades you can go from almost total darkness to allowing the window's full light capacity. Fortunately, there are a great variety of window shades available now, and you have endless decorative possibilities. You can buy bright-colored solid or printed, washable, ready-made shades, or you make your own with fabric and shade cloth. Most can be easily laminated together with an iron. You can glue on trims. You can paint shades or make decorative cutouts on the lower edge. Shade cloth, available in many widths, comes in both room-darkening and translucent densities. Shade shops will custom make shades with the fabric of your choice.

Blinds. The old institutional Venetian blind has been revolutionized. It always supplied the ultimate flexibility in light control, but now it offers decorative appeal as well. The wide-slatted Venetian blind has been streamlined to more sleek, narrow slats. It comes in every color and finish imaginable; you may even use more than one color to suit your design. If you need to cover a large amount of window space, these blinds can add up to quite an investment; they should last forever.

Bamboo shades and woven woods. Bamboo shades are inexpensive and as flexible as fabric shades. Some light does come through them when they are down. If you do not like the naturally-finished shades, you can paint them. They are easy to maintain and should last many years. Woven woods are similar except that they cannot be painted successfully and they cost more.

Shutters. Wooden shutters allow flexible light control, especially if they are hinged so they can be folded away from the window to allow maximum light. When left over a window, with the slats open, they will darken a room. Shutters are a substantial investment but they will last for a long time and require minimal maintenance. You can refinish or repaint them.

Curtains. The most commonly used window covering is the fabric curtain. Curtains are less flexible in controlling light than shutters, shades, or blinds because they are either "open" or "closed" but they have other advantages. They run the gamut from simple gathered cafe curtains to pleated linen drapes. Because their range of style, pattern, color, and texture is limitless, curtains can be the best choice. Price varies greatly according to the fabric and labor involved.

Curtains are less durable than other window coverings. They fade, stain, rip, and wear out. In a child's room they get more wear and tear. Since a child may outgrow the fabric, avoid expensive curtains if your budget is limited.

These are the basic alternatives you have in window coverings. You may choose to combine them—curtains *and* shades, for example. Whatever you decide, try to make your window coverings easy for your child to manage. Can he open the curtains easily? Pull up the blinds? If not, you will have to do it or he will spend his time in semi-darkness.

Window *treatments* are another matter. You may want to make your child's window or windows the center of attention, or you may choose to play them down if they are small, awkwardly located, or have an unappealing view. You can play them down by matching the color of the window covering with the surrounding wall, or matching the curtain pattern with the wall pattern. You can draw attention to the windows by painting graphics around them, using contrasting color for the window covering, stenciling a design around the window, etc. The illustrations in this book show a variety of window treatments.

Probably the most ignored space in any room is the space occupied by the doors. Since you probably will have to accommodate many activities in your child's room, it is wise to use all the available space. Why not put doors to work? For instance, you can paint the back of a door with a blackboard paint and make it a chalk board, or cover it with bulletin board material. Paint a growth stick on your child's door or use hooks to provide extra storage. Mirrors are not recommended for young children, though, for the obvious safety hazards they pose in a child's room.

There are many ways you can make your child's windows and doors both functional and attractive. If you decide to use the window space as an activity area, make certain it is safe. Add window locks and guards if necessary. Consider putting screens on the *inside* if appropriate. You can incorporate your safety measures into your decorative scheme by using a latticework screen, for example. A safe window does not need to be unattractive.

11. If you have windows with an unappealing view but need their light, you might try one of these ideas. With double-hung windows, you can glue a panel of fabric which lets light through on the lower pane, trim the perimeter with ribbon, and install shutters above.

12. *The second window solves the problem by keeping the eye focused inside the room while allowing in a maximum amount of light. Instead of curtains, hang your child's collections in the window—airplanes, mobiles, dolls, plants, etc. Add a shade if you like.*

13. *If you have a small window which is out of proportion with the rest of the room, you can make it appear larger and more interesting by framing it with ceramic tiles, vinyl tiles, or a stenciled border.*

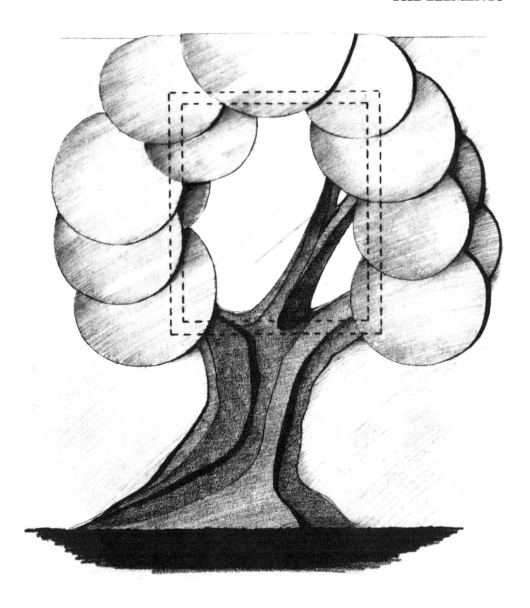

14. *You can even make a small window the major focus of the room. Here a tree cut out of plywood is mounted on the wall over the window providing an especially dramatic and whimsical solution.*

15. Not only can you decorate children's windows, but you can also make good use of window space. Because windows are the source of natural light, the space around a window is ideal for activities such as reading, study, crafts, hobbies, etc. Shown here is a window seat reading nook. You can put book shelves on either side of the window and add a storage seat or bed if the area is large enough. This makes a cozy, inviting place to curl up and read or daydream, and provides extra storage underneath.

16. *This window space is used for a long work center. Plywood arches are mounted on the wall over the windows and painted. Bright colored, narrow blinds provide light control.*

17. *Two desks and a common reading nook share this window space providing plenty of natural light for them all.*

18. *Paint your child's name on the front of her door.*

19. Draw an outline of your child, cut it out of plywood, add dowels, and screw it to the door. Your child now has a personal, handy place to hang coats, shoes, hats, bags, etc.

20. *Doors are sometimes in awkward places. Depending on your needs, you may want to emphasize its presence or make it disappear. Here, you are clearly shown the door.*

21. Incorporating the door as part of the wall surface effectively makes it disappear in this painted wall mural.

22. Turn the back of your child's door into a storage area for letters, books, pencils, etc., by making a shallow box with shelves and smaller boxes inside. Then screw the entire unit to the door.

23. *If you do not have a door and need an inexpensive one, try a bright-colored fabric curtain—also fun for hiding and fantasy play.*

24. *You can also cut the door to your child's room in half. Children love Dutch doors and they can offer an attractive solution to the problem of keeping a young child safely contained at times. Here the child's room becomes a giant playpen where you can keep an eye on things with ease, while your child can be alone without feeling lonely or boxed in.*

25. *If your child is lucky enough to have paneled doors, you can make each panel serve a separate function. Here, the three panels provide a bulletin board, chalkboard, and magnetic board.*

26. *A paneled door to a walk-in closet can make a delightful puppet theater. Just cut out the center panel and add "stage" curtains.*

Furniture

The furniture required by a child is simple: he needs a bed, table or desk space, seating, and storage.

There are two broad areas to consider when selecting children's furniture: where do you get it and what type do you want? You will want to keep your list of priorities in mind as you incorporate the furniture into the total room design. The following are possible sources:

Ready-made furniture. This is the easiest option. Ready-made furniture is available in wood, plastic, lightweight metal, and reinforced cardboard. Some of it is wonderfully innovative. Generally, you pay for what you get. Durability and good design cost more.

If you are prepared to make a major investment and want the furniture to last through childhood, look for two things: *durability* and *adjustability*. Children give their furniture an unbelievable amount of abuse. Keep this in mind whatever you buy, and ask yourself if it is likely to survive. Give prospective buys a detailed inspection and some good prodding, thumping, and pulling. If an item indicates some weakness in your tests, it will not stand up in your child's room.

Remember that children grow. As the scale chart indicates, no one scale will function throughout childhood. If you want to make a long-term investment in furniture, make sure it is adjustable. Can the desk or table height be raised and lowered? Do the bunkbeds come apart so they can be used as twin beds later? Can you stack or rearrange storage units? You will obviously want to avoid miniature, baby-looking furniture that your child will outgrow quickly. Your best bet is furniture that is designed simply so that any age child will feel comfortable with it.

If you do not want to make a large or permanent investment in furniture, durability and adjustability are of less importance. You can get rid of the furniture when it becomes too small or wears out. Some of the new, bright-colored reinforced cardboard furniture is attractive and inexpensive. Your furniture design choices can be more age-related.

The advantages of ready-made new furniture are: it is easy to buy and it can be moved around. Its disadvantages are: it can be costly and inefficient. While most ready-made furniture comes in standardized sizes, children's rooms do not. Fitting ready-made pieces into your child's room may mean wasted space. It may also limit where you can place the furniture.

Unfinished furniture. The major difference between unfinished furniture and new, ready-made furniture is that *you* provide the finish (paint, stain, oils, sealers, polyurethane, etc.) and, usually save money. You do not have as many designs to choose from but you select the exact finish and color you want. In terms of durability, adjustability and size, unfinished furniture offers the same options as ready-made finished furniture.

Used furniture. You can save substantially by buying used furniture. You may need to invest some time and money in repairs and refinishing or painting, but the results are often charming. The drawback of this furniture is that it has been used and may be worn, weakened, or unsafe. Inspect used furniture very carefully for structural weaknesses. Unless it is basically sound, it is not worth buying. It is not wise to furnish a child's room with antiques or objects that can be easily destroyed. If you cannot stand to have an object damaged, put it somewhere else.

Built-in furniture. The attractions of built-in furniture are: it can be exactly what you want, fit the specific requirements of your child's room, and maximize usable space. However, once you have built-ins, they stay in place. You cannot move them around the room or take them with you if you leave. Their cost varies tremendously. If you do the job yourself with inexpensive materials, they may be the least expensive way to furnish your child's room. On the other hand, if you require a paid carpenter, elaborate built-ins can be very expensive.

Built-ins are permanent. Before you decide on them, consult your list of priorities. You probably won't want to devote the time, money, and permanence to built-ins if your child will outgrow them soon or you anticipate moving next year. Adjustability, durablity and flexibility are the key requirements. Materials need not be expensive, but they should be sturdy and safe.

If you choose built-ins, you have the freedom of design and size. Beds do not have to be 39" × 75". You can design your own furniture to fit the available space and thus, use the space more efficiently. Built-ins generally maximize the play area of your child's room.

Homemade furniture. If you have the time and interest, you may want to try to make some furniture. If you select a project appropriate to your skill level, this will not be a difficult undertaking. A sleeping platform or pit consists of plywood boxes covered with foam and fabric or carpeting. Simple desks, tables, and even storage units can be made from a variety of materials. You can make a desk from a plank supported by two storage boxes. With minor alterations and refinishing, discarded electrical cable spools can serve as attractive tables. Brick and board storage shelves are safe for a child's room if you secure them with wooden clothes poles running from floor to ceiling.

Homemade furniture can be the least expensive way to furnish your child's room as well as the most fun and satisfying. You have the same freedom as with built-ins but you have more flexibility. You can move this furniture around. You can take it with you when you move. You can be as elaborate and sophisticated as your skills and imagination allow.

Making furniture is not for everyone, but you may enjoy experimenting with a piece or two. Just keep safety, sturdiness, and durability in mind. Your child won't notice if your efforts aren't perfect.

Combining these options is the most common solution to furnishing a child's room. New ready-made furniture, favorite hand-me-downs, and built-ins can all co-exist happily in a child's room.

When it comes to selecting the type or style of your child's furniture, you have several choices. There are many ways to provide furniture for sleeping, storage, sitting, and working on projects. The furniture can be as simple or elaborate, inexpensive or costly, and temporary or permanent as you want depending on your priorities. If you view the component in terms of its function, you greatly expand your choices. In other words, your child needs a place to sleep. That does not mean he has to have a conventional twin bed with box springs and mattress. A sleep sack on a foam-padded platform works just as well. Likewise, a child's need for clothes and toy storage does not limit you to a chest of drawers. With this in mind, here are some of your options.

Tables, desks, and seating. A pre-school child may not require a desk but he will need some kind of table for games, playdough, crafts, etc. It doesn't have to be expensive or complicated. Your choices include:

- Standard round, square, or rectangular wood tables.

- Molded plastic tables.

- Spool tables.

- Stacking tables.

- Wood or reinforced cardboard box tables.

When a child begins school, he will need work space. Generally, as a child grows older, he needs more large, uncluttered space for study, hobbies, and crafts. A table can suffice for some time. In fact, there may not be a clear distinction between table and desk if the table is large enough. For desks, your choices include: wood, metal, plastic laminate, free-standing, built-in, or pull-down. A desk need not be complicated: a wood plank or door supported by two storage units is a perfectly adequate desk.

You can provide seating with standard wooden or plastic chairs, stools, benches, boxes, or stacking chairs. Floor cushions, bean bag chairs, and inflatable chairs also supply informal seatings. Chairs used for study or time-consuming hobbies and crafts, however, should be straightbacked for back support and healthy posture. Children are more alert, less fatigued, and better able to concentrate when they sit with back straight and feet flat on the floor in a sturdy, comfortable chair. This way you encourage healthy posture and good study habits early.

Do not forget scale. It is more important that your child's desk or table and chairs be in proper scale than anything else in his room. When he sits in his chair, his feet should be flat on the floor and his lower and upper legs at right angles with about six to eight inches between the chair seat and table top. Check the scale charts for specific measurements.

Storage furniture. You can solve storage problems with furniture other than the conventional chest of drawers. You may like the idea of a free-standing wardrobe. Trunks provide good storage and double as seating if a pad or cushion are put on top. Pressboard stacking modules can be mixed and matched to provide a very adaptable storage system. You can buy beds which have built-in storage underneath.

Even the free-standing chest of drawers comes in a range of shapes, styles, and sizes these days. You might decide to use the smaller chest-of-drawer units which can be put side-by-side or stacked on top of each other rather than one large piece. You can move them around for variety. If you move, they give you more options in your child's new room.

It is usually an advantage in a child's room to make furniture serve more than one purpose. The storage bed is one space-saving example because the space under beds is often wasted. You can maximize the use of storage furniture by buying or making units which are low enough that their tops can double as work surfaces. Sturdy and tough-finished storage units such as the pressboard stacking modules can be arranged together to provide delightful climbing and jumping structures.

Whatever you select, keep safety in mind. If there is some danger that a chest of drawers can fall over on a child, bolt it to the wall. If the drawers can be pulled out on top of small toes, add drawer stops.

Beds. At age two, children spend about fourteen hours a day sleeping. Most twelve-year-olds spend ten hours a day in bed. The basic requirements for such an important place are quite simple:

- Your child's bed should be large enough that it's not constrictive.

- The mattress should be firm.

- It should be low enough that your child can't be injured by falling out of it, or if necessary, a physical restraint such as a railing should be added to prevent this.

These requirements are generally easy to satisfy. Standard twin beds are more than sufficiently roomy. In fact, you may choose a narrower or shorter bed for your child. Consult the scale chart in this book to give yourself some idea of average growth rates for children.

Doctors recommend firm mattresses for children to encourage muscle and bone development. A firm mattress doesn't have to be expensive. You can buy three- or four-inch polyurethane foam mattresses cut to any size and shape you want. These mattresses are firm but comfortable, and a workable alternative to an expensive box spring and mattress set. Foam is lightweight, portable, and non-allergenic. Most commercial mattresses are made of polyurethane foam: you can save money by making your own.

Making a bed safe isn't difficult. If you have any doubts, add some kind of restraint. You can buy adjustable guard rails to fit most beds, or you can make something yourself. One caution: be sure that the rails are close enough together that your child can't wedge his head between them.

Keeping these considerations in mind, you can choose from several types of beds. Water beds are not recommended for children because they can be easily damaged or punctured and are not sufficiently firm.

Conventional twin beds. These standard beds consist of a frame, box springs, and mattress. They may have a headboard and footboard. Twin beds are readily available and use standard bedding. If you purchase a used twin bed for your child, check the condition and firmness of the mattress. Double beds are not necessary for children's rooms. Children do not need so much sleeping room, and double beds occupy space that can be used more effectively for other activities.

Storage bin beds. These beds are a popular choice for small rooms because they provide storage underneath. They are usually slightly higher than the conventional twin bed. Since they omit the box spring, they supply a generous area for storage drawers. They are available in the standard twin size.

Trundle beds. These are a variation of storage bin beds, except that instead of storage underneath, there is another bed which can be pulled out like a drawer. Trundle beds are an efficient way to sleep overnight friends, but are less satisfactory in permanent room-sharing situations.

Hanging beds. These are an intriguing do-it-yourself alternative which can be made most simply by suspending a sturdy plywood sheet from the ceiling and putting a mattress on top. Not all ceilings will work for this purpose, and special attention should be given to anchoring the bed securely. Hanging beds free floor space, delight children, and cost little. Hang the bed low and raise it as the child grows.

Built-in beds, sleeping pits, and bed platforms. These custom-made beds are inexpensive if you supply the labor. They can be space-savers and wonderful play centers, as well, depending on your design. While most are made to fit a particular room, you can design a bed of this variety which can be moved easily.

Pull-down or Murphy beds. If your child has a Murphy bed in his room already, you may want to keep it because it's a space-saver. Installing a new Murphy bed however, can be extremely expensive and complicated. You might want to consider it if your child's room is very small and you intend to remain in your home for a long time. A homemade pull-down bed is a less expensive alternative.

Bunk beds. A classic favorite for children's rooms, bunk beds economize space and provide an outlet for a child's urge to climb. Although they are usually found in rooms which children share, they can be useful for one child. They offer extra sleeping space for guests and the extra bunk can be turned into a play area when not in use.

There are four basic types of bunk beds. The most common is the two-bunk permanent bed. (The beds do not come apart to form two twin beds.) The second type consists of single beds which can be stacked on top of each other up to three levels high. A third variety consists of free-standing beds with adjustable legs so that you can place one bed at right angles under the other for an L-shaped system. The fourth one, which is fairly new, is a highly innovative bunk bed. It is attached to the wall and folds up during the day to an eleven inch deep unit with a blackboard surface—an excellent space-saving design.

Since bunk beds are used most commonly in shared rooms, the section on sharing a room in Chapter 3 contains several illustrations and ideas. If you decide on bunk beds, you should have no problem with availability. Styles range from old-fashioned wood spindle types to "space-age" cylindrical varieties. It is generally unwise for children under the age of five to sleep on the top bunk.

Bedding. Bed-making is one of those daily chores that is a part of your child's general room maintenance. Who is going to make the bed? If you child is responsible, you should keep it simple. You do not have to use a bottom sheet, top sheet, blankets and bedspread as bed clothes.

Try a variation of the European system with a fitted bottom sheet and a colorful, washable comforter on top. A sleep sack is another easy-maintenance option. You can either buy or make a sleeping bag out of light-weight, washable, quilted or insulated fabric. It is attractive and easy to take care of. Whatever bedding you select, consider its qualities of durability, wrinkle-resistance, and launderability. Many of the new designs in easy-care sheets are so colorful and attractive that you might want to incorporate the fabric elsewhere in your child's room.

Making a bed more than a bed. Most beds occupy a fair amount of the total space in a child's room. Even though children spend half their childhood asleep, the other half is full of a myriad of activities that demand space. If you can make your child's bed more than a place to sleep, so much the better.

One of the easiest ways to add a little magic to your child's bed is through the use of fabric. Tents and canopies enchant children. They love places to hide, to pretend, to daydream. You don't need to be a skilled seamstress to give your child's bed a touch of fantasy. The following illustrations are all simple and inexpensive.

The ideas and illustrations in this chapter are by no means exhaustive. They are included to suggest some of the diverse ways you can treat a child's bed and to stimulate your own ideas. Children are usually very attached to their beds, so it is especially satisfying to make them inviting places.

27. *This strip canopy can be very colorful and eye-catching. Attach one wooden clothes pole rod at the top of the wall with two screw-in hooks and the other one on the ceiling the same way. Run strips of fabric up the wall and over the ceiling rods, attaching them to the rods if necessary.*

28. *A sleeping pit is basically a box or platform with a hole in the center. You create a "pit" by artificially raising the floor. A sleeping pit can be built-in or free-standing and covered with carpeting, floor tile, or paint. Put a mattress and some pillows in the pit. It is not only a bed, but a place to climb, jump, sit, play, curl up and read, etc.*

29. Here is an idea which satisfies all a child's basic furniture requirements in one system. It is a large U-shaped construction which frees
the center of the room for play. Low storage units are placed around the
walls with plywood screwed on top, providing a giant desk and work
surface. The beds consist of ¾-inch foam mattresses which sit on top
of the plywood but can be removed if the surface is needed for other
activities. Since it is not built-in, it can be easily disassembled and
reassembled.

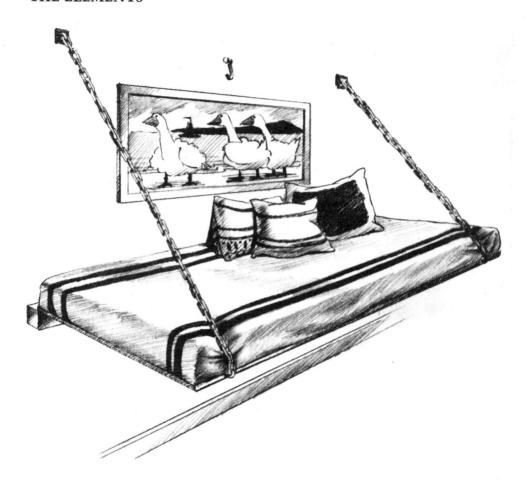

30. This pull down bed can be made easily and inexpensively by nailing a 2 x 4 length of wood to the wall and attaching a piece of plywood to it with continuous piano hinges or several heavy hinges. Sturdy chain runs from hooks in the wall to screw eyes in the plywood platform for support on the other side. You can paint the bottom of the plywood with chalkboard paint or make it a bulletin board which can be used when the bed is up. An unobtrusive hook or latch above the picture on the wall can secure the bed when it is up.

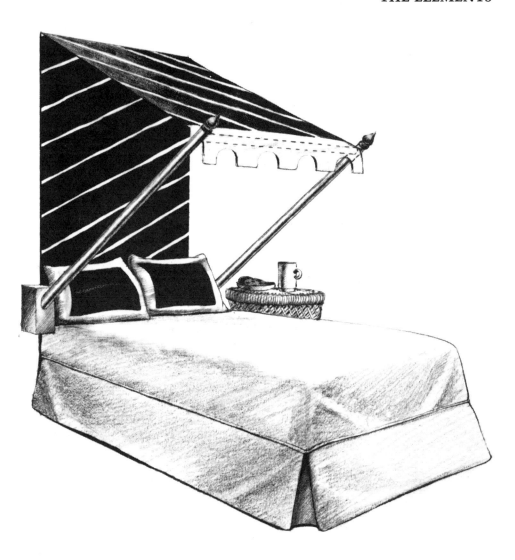

31. *This simple awning looks like a campaign tent but can provide other inspiration for a child's rich imagination. Run clothes pole "spears" into wood blocks attached to the wall. Add a crosspiece at the top for support. The "spear tips" are ready-made, screw-on, decorative wood end pieces for curtain poles. Run the fabric up the wall and attach with staples, double-sided tape, or Velcro. Drape over the crosspiece and attach if necessary.*

32. *You can make this simple tent by running a clothes pole the length of the bed and suspending it from the ceiling with a screw eye and chain, or screw hooks. Sew a couple of sheets together, run the fabric over the pole, and attach the bottom edges to the floor or wall with Velcro. If you want to put a small piece of Velcro mid-way up the wall, you can fold the tent flaps back to provide easy access to the bed.*

33. Make your daughter's bed a bower of flowers with one long panel of fabric attached to the ceiling with staples, Velcro, or double-sided tape. Paint matching flowers in the wall and make some green, leaf pillows. You might also want to add a "petal" bedspread.

34. This romantic canopy can be assembled in fifteen minutes. Screw five large rings into the ceiling—one above each corner of the bed and one directly above the center of the bed. Then, take two long lengths of fabric. Run one length through a corner ring, through the center ring, and through the opposite corner ring and let drop to the floor. Do the same with the remaining fabric and the remaining rings.

35. An easy canopy bed idea consists of covering a square of plywood with fabric, attaching a length of fabric at each corner, and letting the fabric drape down to the bed posts. Screw the plywood to the ceiling.

36. *You can make an easy cornice by covering a box with fabric and screwing it to the ceiling. Attach fabric to the inside of the box for tie-back curtains, if you like.*

37. If you have an old-fashioned romantic on your hands, this idea provides a frilly spot to daydream. Buy a semi-circular curtain rod and attach it to the wall. Then add "curtains" which can be pulled back around the bed posts. Add all the bows, ruffles, lace, and fluffy pillows you want.

38. For a cozy feeling, take two lengths of wooden clothes pole and screw one end into the wall while the other end is suspended from the ceiling with screw eyes and chain. Run a panel of fabric over both poles.

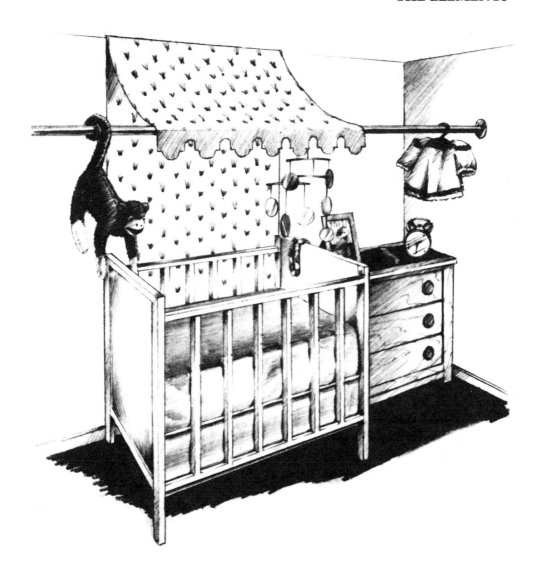

39. *This roof awning can give an infant something colorful to look up at. Screw closet pole holders to opposite walls and have wooden closet poles cut to length. Then simply run a width of fabric up the wall, attach at the ceiling joint with staples, double-sided tape, or Velcro, and drape the decorative edge over the pole. The rest of the pole can be used to hang mobiles, toys, and other visually stimulating items for the crib-bound.*

40. *Delight your child with a special headboard. Children love to see their names, so why not at the head of their bed? This headboard can either be painted on the wall or cut out of plywood and painted or upholstered with fabric and screwed to the wall. If the bed already has a headboard, the letters can probably be attached to it.*

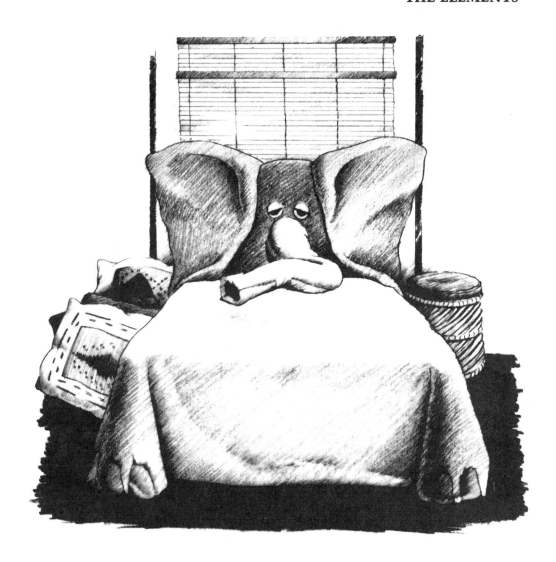

41. Even a plain old headboard can be given whimsical charm by adding a few stick-ons. Here, pillow ears and a stuffed tube trunk can be attached with Velcro to enable easy removal for laundering or other use. You can cut stick-on eyes from vinyl press-on paper. If your child gets weary of the beast, you can quickly make him disappear.

42. *You can hang this delightful appliqued, quilted headboard from the wall or add it to the existing frame. Take one of your child's favorite works of art and copy it on fabric with appliques in differing fabric patterns. Stuff it slightly and machine- or hand-quilt it sufficiently so that the stuffing does not bunch at the bottom. Hang it with tabs or loops of fabric.*

43. *This rainbow headboard can be cut out of plywood and painted or upholstered, or painted right on the wall. It takes on a third dimension if you add a circular pillow in the center.*

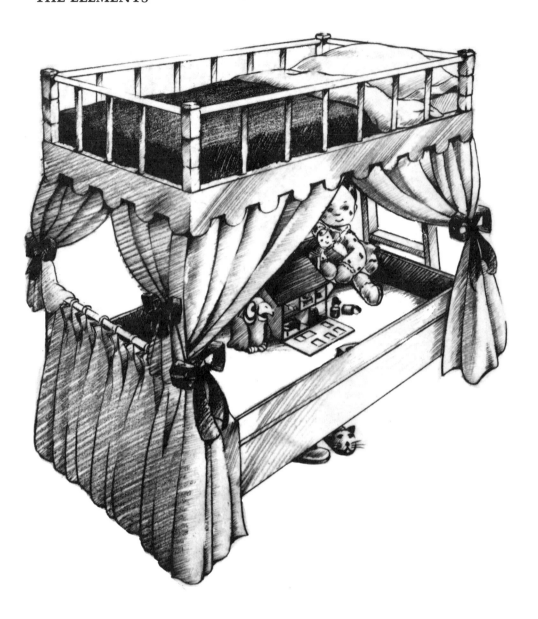

44. If you have bunk beds, but only one child in the room, put the unused bunk to work. Here the upper bunk is used for sleeping and the lower bunk turned into a playhouse using only fabric and curtain rods. You could also cover the sides of the bottom bunk with plywood sheets with doors and windows cut out. If you remove the box springs and mattress from the lower bunk and replace them with a sheet of plywood, you have even more play space.

Storage

Have you ever noticed that a child's room never seems to have enough storage? All of the activities and their accompanying paraphernalia compete for space. The standard size closet and chest of drawers are frequently insufficient. As a result, children's rooms become disorganized and messy very quickly. A child may get frustrated trying to find an item in the general chaos. At the end of a long, tiring day, you may look at your child's room and feel equally overwhelmed.

There are no magic solutions to this problem; it is an unavoidable and essential by-product of learning and growing up. But you can organize the storage in your child's room to minimize the chaos and enable a child to put his own things away.

Open storage. If you make sure the shelving is at your child's level, open shelving encourages toy organiztion. Your child can see where everything belongs and return things to their place. Since your child can look at his toys, he is more likely to play with them. Open storage gives a room warmth and personality but too much can be busy and distracting. You may want to rotate a few toys at a time. You can put a collection of currently ignored toys in the garage or basement. Every few months change toys. Children greet them like long-lost friends, and you have simplified pickup problems by taking some toys out of circulation.

If, for one reason or another, you must have some open storage which is not in your child's reach, use if for the least desirable items. When favorite toys are out of reach but within view, a child is tempted to climb to them. For convenience as well as safety, items that are used frequently should be the easiest to reach.

There are many kinds of open storage. Standard and bracket shelving is popular because it allows you to move shelves around and create your own wall system. You can also build a simple storage system yourself.

Closets. Probably the largest space in your child's room that can be devoted soley to storage is the closet. If you prefer having toys and games accessible to your child but out of sight, make the most of your closet. Shelving can be added to most closets. Dressers, stacking bins, baskets and box modules can sometimes fit, too.

The clothes pole in the standard closet is much too high for children, so consider adding another at a lower level or purchasing an adjustable pole extender which hangs from the original pole. This extender will increase the clothes hanging surface and make it possible for your child to reach his clothes easily. To encourage your child to be self-sufficient and dress himself, his clothes should be readily accessible. Hooks on the backs of closet doors or inside the closet itself provide a simple means for young children to hang their clothing.

Miscellaneous storage. Closets and shelving provide large areas of storage, but children also need places to put smaller items. Puzzle pieces, "leggos", little people, small cars and animals tend to get lost when lumped together with larger toys. These small items need separate storage if they are to be used and enjoyed. Here are a few storage ideas for small items and larger toys.

- Buy your coffee in three pound cans and spray paint them bright colors when they are empty. On the outside of the can draw a picture of the contents along with the word. Even if they can't read yet, children can easily recognize what is in the can and put things away.

- Clear plastic shoe boxes will hold small items and allow children to see exactly what is inside.

- Cardboard file boxes available at stationery or office supply stores provide storage and come with content labels.

- Baskets provide inexpensive toy storage. If you would like to anchor them off the floor, hang them with fabric flaps over a clothes pole.

- Plastic dish bins can be used as removable drawers in an easy-to-make system which supports them on the side. Heavy-duty colorful plastic bins are available at restaurant supply stores.

- Mailboxes make intriguing containers for toys or supplies.

- Fiber or cardboard drums painted bright colors can accommodate a large assortment of toys and can also be used as caves or tunnels when empty.

- You can use the space under the bed to store rolling drawers on casters.

- A toy bin seat serves two functions in one. Just make sure the lid is easy for your child to manage.

- Three-tiered wire baskets provide inexpensive hanging storage.

- Wood or fiberboard boxes can be used for play during the day and filled with toys at night.

- Hat boxes trimmed with fabric and ribbon make an attractive storage addition to a room.

- Toy storage wagons will hold toys as well as children, and they can be pulled around easily.

Taking toys, clothes, games, and hobbies out and putting them away becomes time-consuming over the course of a day. Trying to find something in a crowded room is a frustrating task. Thoughtful organization and well-chosen storage arrangements save you and your child time and aggravation.

45. Here is one idea that consists of three wooden ladders and assorted size boards. You can move the boards around to fit your child's changing storage needs, provide an adjustable desk surface, and give your child a safe place to climb.

46. Open storage does not need to be limited to shelving. Here assorted boxes and items are mounted on plywood to furnish toy storage, bulletin board, book shelves, and desk. Take advantage of irregularly shaped walls by making an irregularly shaped wall unit. This one can be used indefinitely if you change the items to be displayed and stored as your child grows.

47. *This small closet makes the maximum use of available space by adding shelving, a clothes pole extender, hooks and shoe bag on the back of the door, and several of the storage ideas discussed in this section.*

Lighting

Lighting is an important and subtle element in a child's room. Harsh lighting can change the entire effect of an otherwise inviting room and cause a child to feel vaguely uncomfortable. He may not know why he feels better taking his toys and playing somewhere else. Dim or muted light will strain his eyes and make it impossible to undertake certain activities.

A child's room requires a lighting system designed to enhance the activities that take place there: it needs both general and specific light. You need overall illumination for the room and specific light sources for activities like reading, studying and playing with games.

Use one or more lamps, wall-mounted fixtures, or ceiling fixtures as a source of general light. Since wall or ceiling fixtures frequently give off an unpleasantly direct light, you might want to consider adding a globe or shade to soften the effect and diffuse the light. Fluorescent light is not recommended for general illumination because of its harshness.

Specific light for reading and desk work can be supplied by table lamps, lamps with movable arms, hanging lamps, wall-mounted lamps, tensor lamps, and fluorescent tubes under shelves. Provide some lighting near a child's bed for reading and convenience when he gets up at night. Make sure there is enough light so your child never strains his eyes.

Glare from an unshielded light bulb can quickly cause eye strain. Select reading or study lamps carefully to avoid glare. Gooseneck, pulldown, drafting lamps, or any lamps with movable arms can be easily adjusted to the proper height and position.

Safety considerations are particularly important when choosing the lighting for your child's room. Avoid putting lamps in locations where a child can burn himself. Lamps that are hung or mounted permanently are good for young children because they cannot be knocked over. Be aware of lamps such as floor lamps that tip easily and pay strict attention to bulb wattage. If a lamp specifies use of a 60-watt bulb, it may be dangerous to use one with a larger wattage. Be sure to cover unused electrical outlets and avoid using extension cords in the rooms of young children.

You will find a vast array of lamps and lighting fixtures for sale today, but you can also make your own quite easily and inexpensively. Wiring a lamp is not difficult. Ask someone knowledgeable if you feel uncertain. The major problem in making your own lamp is the amount of heat to which the shade is exposed. Take care with shades that may burn or melt, and experiment to see what the maximum wattage should be. You can use all kinds of objects to make a lamp. The illustrations show a few you are likely to find around the house.

Whether you purchase lamps or make them, remember to provide adequate light and make sure the lamps are safe. The natural light of day may be enough to illuminate most of your young child's activities now, but as he grows older (and stays up later), he will need more specific light sources. Lighting should be as carefully thought-out and planned as any other part of your child's room.

48. This drawing illustrates the proper relationship between reading light source and eye level. A child should not be able to see a lamp's light bulb while seated at his desk or reading in bed.

49. *All five of these hanging lamps begin with a simple cord, socket, and globe light bulb. Let your imagination go; you can make a lampshade from almost anything. This illustration shows a bright laminate salad bowl, a basket, gathered fabric over a lampshade frame, a hat, and an umbrella.*

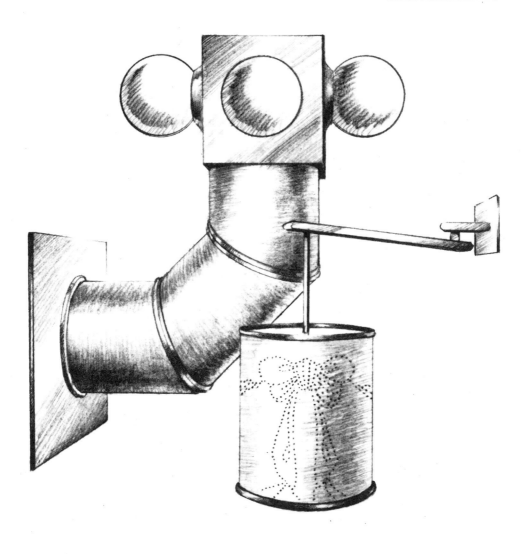

50. You can also make lighting fixtures out of spray-painted aluminum venting pipe with wiring and sockets inside and bulb outside. Transform a coffee can with paint and a design punched out with a puncturing tool to allow light through.

3
Special Problems

If your situation is somewhat different: don't worry. Here are some ideas to help you deal with some of those special problems like designing a nursery or a shared room, or a room in a rented home.

The Nursery

Babies begin to crawl at differing ages, varying from six to ten months. The term often used to describe an infant's quarters during this period is "the nursery". As you can see, the nursery is a short-lived affair, and for this reason a special challenge.

You need not panic about where your newborn is going to live, or feel pressured to move to larger quarters. An infant's demands of his environment are incredibly simple. He needs fresh air, a comfortable temperature range, light, and a place to sleep. Mainly, an infant needs you. You are the sole nurturer at this stage; so arrange things for your comfort and ease.

An infant does not require his own room. Indeed, it may be a real inconvenience for you to run back and forth from his room to other parts of the house. You may prefer to keep him in a baby buggy or a bassinet on casters and roll him around to where you are. If he's napping, you can roll him to a quiet spot in the house, (though there is evidence that newborns are often soothed by noise rather than disturbed by it). At night you can roll your baby to a spot which is far enough to allow you to sleep undisturbed but near enough to hear his cries if he wakes. A portable room provides freedom and easy access for you; it gives your baby comfort in being close to you and your familiar sounds.

There are other alternatives to a full-sized room. You may have an unused niche in the house that is just the right size. You can transform a walk-in closet with a window into a delightful nursery. Make sure the window works so the baby will have fresh air. Extra bathrooms can also be converted into nurseries, and are quite handy because the sink and washing paraphernalia are nearby. Remember to do any painting several weeks before a baby actually occupies a room or nook to avoid the danger of toxic fumes.

You might want to combine a fully-equipped nursery and some way to keep your infant close to you at times. As the following illustrations show, an infant does not require much space. He just needs a lot of love.

Cribs. Most people invest in a crib. A child usually outgrows a crib by age three (sometimes earlier). Your crib should be strong enough to withstand the beating it will receive during these vigorous early years. If you are purchasing a crib for your first child and intend to have more children, invest in a crib which is sturdy and designed to last. Used cribs are sometimes good buys, but check them over very carefully. A crib should have a side which raises and lowers, and an adjustable bed height. Examine the rails to make sure they are spaced closely enough to each other that a baby cannot wedge his head between them. A bumper guard is good no matter what style of crib you choose. The mattress should be firm.

A newborn, however, does not need a crib. A crib may be too big for him. The newborn usually prefers the security of being enclosed. Perhaps because young parents are realizing the wisdom of their grandparents, the cradle is becoming popular again.

The cradle is a classic device tailored to meet a newborn's needs. It is small so it gives the infant a sense of security. Its rocking motion lulls and soothes him. In addition, a cradle is convenient for the parent. You can move it from room to room with relative ease. You can set it on the floor and rock it with your foot while your hands are otherwise occupied. If you hang it and give it a slight push, it will sway gently for a long, lulling time. If you don't have the money to buy a cradle or the time and skill to make one, see if you can borrow one from friends or relatives. A cradle tends to be one of those treasured family possessions that most people love to lend.

The cradle is not the only alternative to a crib for the newborn. Baskets and bassinets are popular, but even a box or drawer will suffice.

Newborns are not choosy, but they do grow quickly. By the time your infant begins to kick his arms and legs out and attempts to roll over (three to five months), he is ready for roomier quarters. Be prepared to move your baby to a crib or a larger sleeping space at this time.

All the other furniture typically found in a nursery is more for you than your infant, so suit yourself. You will need someplace to store all the paraphernalia that goes with changing clothes and diapers. It does not necessarily have to be located in the nursery if it's more convenient for you to change your baby elsewhere. For the same reason, a bathing or changing table is not essential unless you really want one. Actually, it is much safer to change a squirming baby on the floor. Light weight plastic infant baby basins which can be carried to the water source are much more practical than most bathing table arrangements.

Seasoned parents strongly recommend a comfortable chair for the mother. Whether you breast-feed or bottle-feed your infant, you will need something to sit in which supports your back and arms. You are going to spend a great deal of time in this position during the first few months. The classic, of course, is the rocker, and a truly comfortable rocker is probably the best choice you can make. It's soothing to you and your infant.

The senses are the focus of an infant's development in this period. His sense of touch, taste, smell and hearing are stimulated and satisfied mainly by you—your touch, your smell, your voice, and the taste of the milk you provide. Adding visual stimulation to your baby's quarters encourages his development; even newborns respond to color and movement. Mobiles are popular because their slow movement will engross a baby for a long period of time. Hang mobiles and other colorful objects low over your baby's bed so they are within his range of focus.

The nursery does not need to be a major investment of time or money. In fact, it does not need to be a room at all. Since all an infant needs is a safe, comforting place to sleep, fresh air, warmth, light, and visual stimulation, what you choose should make things easier and more comfortable for you. After all, what an infant needs most are happy, relaxed parents.

51. *A small walk-in closet with a window for ventilation and light can serve as perfectly adequate quarters for a newborn. Hang a cradle from the ceiling and soothe your baby with its gently rocking motion.*

52. *Closet space under a stairway may be just the right size for a crib and dresser. Hang mobiles and toys from the sloping ceiling and add bright colored window covering. Your baby can have a charming "room" on his own scale.*

53. *Extra bathrooms can be magically transformed into wonderful nurseries too. Here an old alcove bathtub is covered with a sheet of plywood, a foam mattress set on top, and a guard rail added. The bed doubles as a changing table with the convenience of a sink just steps away.*

54. Another bathroom alternative is to cover the tub with a sheet of plywood and set a cradle, basket, or portacrib on top. Shelving can be added to the back for diapers, supplies, and toys. Tie-back curtains complete this charming and handy nursery alcove.

Sharing a Room

Trying to fit two or more children and all their belongings into one space requires some real ingenuity. You want to avoid chaos and claustrophobia and give your children some place to play. When you put two or more personalities together in very close quarters, you must balance each child's need for space and privacy.

Children who share a room are going to have plenty of company and togetherness. Designs for shared rooms often fail to take children's needs for privacy into account. The need for privacy is more intense for certain children and at certain ages, but all children need to retreat once in a while. If you don't provide some kind of privacy for your children, they will inevitably do it themselves, often in a less successful manner. Some children draw an imaginary line across the room defining their territories. Others argue about what belongs to whom. You will avoid some of these battles if you include some personal space where a child can go when he wants to be alone.

How you take privacy into account will depend on the intensity of your children's needs for separate space and the permanence of the arrangement. If room sharing is a long-term arrangement for two highly private children, consider some kind of permanent partition which divides one room into two separate rooms. Not all rooms are amenable to this kind of partitioning, and you may have to consult an expert about problems of light, heat, and air circulation. On the other hand, a panel of fabric hanging between two beds may provide sufficient privacy if the children's needs for privacy are minimal, or if room sharing is temporary.

The easiest and most logical place to provide some privacy is around the beds. A child's bed may be the only spot in the room which belongs to him alone. You can place some kind of divider *between* the beds. This divider can be simple or elaborate, permanent or temporary depending on your needs. Here are a few ideas:

- Place a folding screen between the beds. You can either make one by hinging three frames together and stapling on fabric or buy one. Either way, it is easy to move around.

- Separate your children's beds with some kind of storage divider: bookcases, shelving, cabinets, dressers, etc.

- Make a plywood divider that is either built-in or in a frame on casters. You can surface it for a bulletin board, or cut out mail slots and windows for play, or create a two-way puppet theater for mutual entertainment.

- Hang cargo netting between two beds. It is a subtle see-through divider that accommodates climbing activities.

- Install a ceiling track for more permanent wooden or vinyl accordion dividers, or hang curtains or panels of fabric from them.

- Use a fabric tent or canopy idea illustrated earlier in this book. Most can be used to provide privacy in a shared room.

- Mount window shades from the ceiling between the beds. They can be raised or lowered as the situation requires.

- Use a desk or work counter as a divider. For more privacy, add a low or ceiling-high partition out of pegboard or plywood.

You can also arrange the beds to create privacy for your children. The use of alternate space often works as effectively as an actual divider. You may combine the bed placement and a divider for more privacy. Here are a few ways to place beds for maximum privacy.

- The classic bunk bed provides privacy by dividing space into upper and lower areas. When both children are in bed, they cannot see each other.

- If you have two beds, one of which can be raised, you can create an L-shaped variation of the bunk bed. The upper bunk goes lengthwise along one wall and the lower bunk fits at right angles underneath, against the other wall creating an L-shape. This solution provides privacy like a bunk bed and allows you to use the corner.

- You may choose to make a sleeping platform for your children and provide privacy by varying the levels.

- Placing twin beds at right angles with a parsons table between in a corner creates an L-shape on the same level. This placement supplies minimal privacy, however, and you may want to add some kind of divider as well.

- If your ceiling is high enough, you might want to add a loft. Lofts are a permanent and relatively inexpensive way to build privacy into a room.

In addition to, or instead of bed space, you may give each child his own desk space, storage area, closet or shelf, depending on what is available. Children need space for a few treasured possessions they don't want to share all the time. The degree of possessiveness varies from child to child and from age to age. Consider how you wish to handle the issue of "ownership" and to what extent you want to accommodate it.

Some space saving ideas. Unless your children share a really large room, you will probably have some difficulty finding places to put everything and sufficient floor space for play as well. It is particularly important to maximize floor space in a shared room because not enough space can limit activities and cause feelings of tension. Space saving ideas have been mentioned throughout this book but it is useful to list them altogether.

- Keep furniture at a minimum and make everything in the room serve several functions.

- Make use of the ceiling.

- Use wall-hung shelves and storage wherever possible.

- Consider bunk beds, built-ins, and lofts—all classic conservers of space. The wall-mounted fold-up bunk bed is a fantastic new space saver.

- Use some of the storage and activity ideas mentioned earlier to put your doors to work.

- Organize closets carefully and efficiently.

- If you use twin beds, place them lengthwise against walls. Placing twin beds outwards from the middle of walls wastes space. If bed-making is difficult with this arrangement, consider one of the easy-maintenance bedding ideas discussed earlier. Floor space is more important.

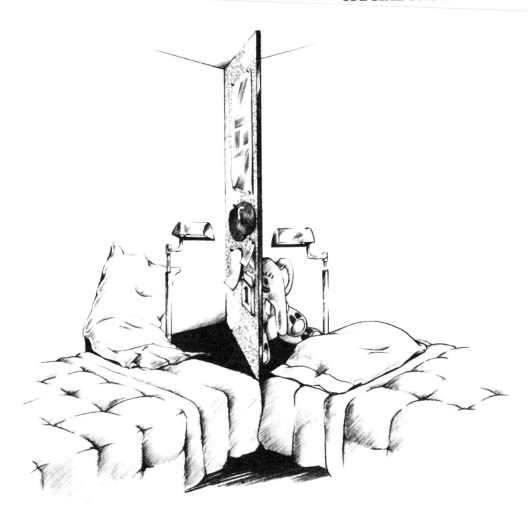

55. Two twin beds can be placed at right angles separated by a parsons table. Adding a plywood bulletin board divider diagonally from the table to the ceiling will give each child some privacy, a place to put a few personal treasures, and control over their own light.

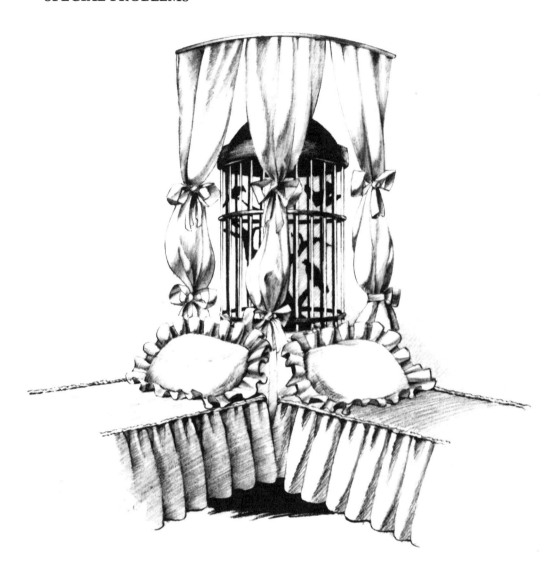

56. *A large bird cage, plants, and an easy "canopy" over the same* parsons table creates a variation of the same arrangement. A standard *semi-circular curtain rod is attached to the ceiling and three widths of* *fabric tied at intervals hang down. The divider is subtle, but does* *provide privacy.*

57. You may choose to omit the parsons table and create a cozy little play pit by adding pillows. Running a post up to the ceiling from the meeting corner of the two beds and hanging fabric from the ceiling insures privacy. When the pit needs light, the curtain can be tied back to the post. Otherwise, the curtains can hang straight down creating privacy, a headboard, and a dark spooky hiding place in the pit.

58. In this room shared by a boy and a girl, each child has a mini-room of his own. The ladder tied into the wall and ceiling accommodates climbing and gymnastic activity. It may be used to suspend toys, plants, mobiles, etc. A bookcase with alternating opening to each side functions as a headboard and provides total privacy and storage. The personalized bedside rugs are cut from carpet remnants.

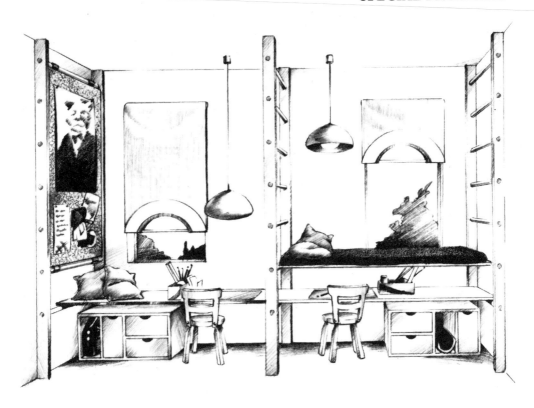

59. *Three floor-to-ceiling wide ladders support this adjustable, space conserving system. The beds consist of sheet plywood with a foam mattress and sleep sack on top (or you may make a lightweight webbed frame instead). The beds hook over the ladder rungs and may be raised during the day, the underside serving as a bulletin board or chalkboard. Each child has his own desk area consisting of a simple plank which can be raised to a higher rung as he grows. A storage unit will fit underneath and lamps can be raised or lowered to proper height for both bed and desk use. The central ladder structure can also be used for climbing and jumping when the beds are up and the loose plank desk removed.*

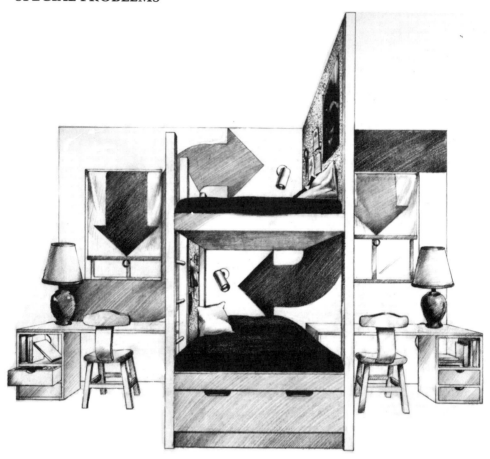

60. Bunk beds are not only space-savers, but also can be used as dividers. The bunk bed here separates the area into two private "rooms" without the problems of air and heat circulation that a permanent partition might create. You can easily make this system using any standard bunk bed and screwing on plywood bulletin board walls. Each child has his own miniature room complete with desk, chair, storage, lighting, and bed. Using different colors on each side will further personalize the space.

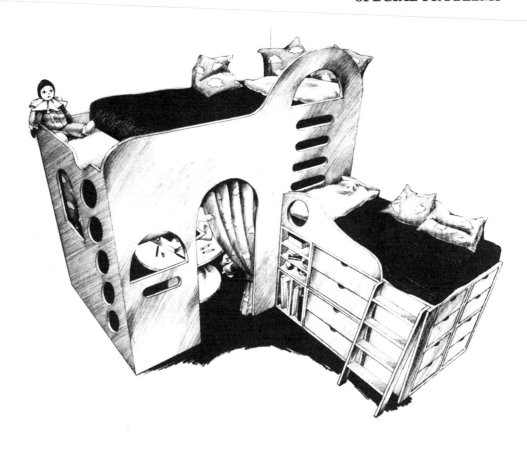

61. *This corner bunk system is not as complex as it may appear. The lower bunk is simply a sheet of plywood and a foam mattress set on top of a variety of pressboard storage modules. The upper bunk is a plywood platform supported by 2 x 4's and 3 x 3 posts. This simple structure is then faced with plywood cut-outs which are screwed onto it. The result is a system which provides sleeping for two, ample storage, plenty of climbing spaces, and a playhouse underneath. Another plus is the relatively small amount of floor space used.*

101

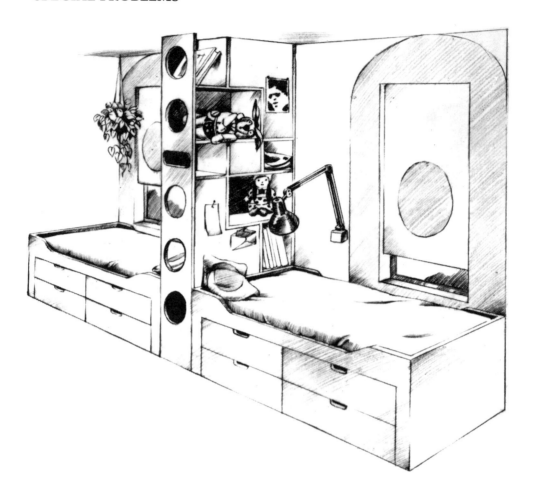

62. Two storage-bin beds provide enough height that these beds also become cozy window seats. A central floor to ceiling bookcase divider with alternate openings on each side insure privacy and allow for storage of personal items. The circles on the side of the bookcase are for climbing.

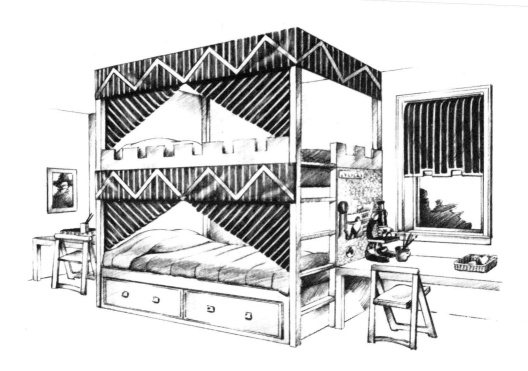

63. *Placing a bunk bed lengthwise along a wall between two windows leaves space for two desk nooks and frees more floor space for play than if it were placed out from the wall. Adding a fabric or plywood headboard-wall at the alternate ends of each bunk will make each desk nook entirely private. For total retreat or fantasy play, campaign tent flaps can be let down.*

103

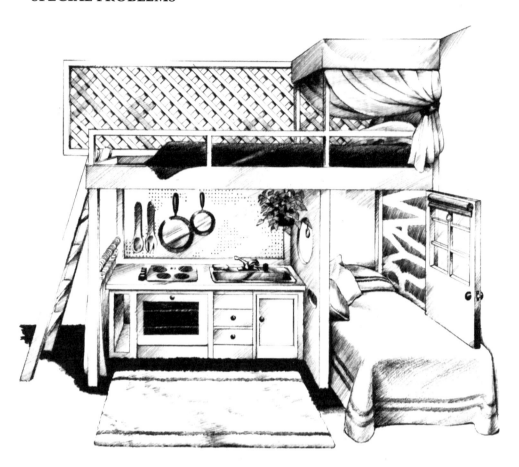

64. *Two free-standing bunk beds can also provide privacy and save space in a small room shared by a boy and a girl. Here the upper bunk is placed high against the wall with a latticework screen against the window for protection. The easy box cornice idea is used for the upper bunk. The lower bunk is set at right angles and given its own wall—a plywood sheet with window cut-outs. By adding a low curtain and a toy stove, the remainder of the space under the upper bunk becomes a cozy play kitchen.*

Ideas for Those Who Rent or Move Frequently

Our society is a highly mobile one. Many families rent rather than own a home. These circumstances pose certain limitations that merit special discussion. The ideas in this section may appeal to you even if you do not rent or move frequently.

If you rent, your landlord may disapprove of any plans which involve nailing or screwing into walls, ceilings, and doors, or he may restrict your color options. You may have to live with the existing flooring. You may be able to avoid most of these restrictions with liberal landlords or long-term leases, but most renters do have their choices limited in some ways.

If you move often, your limitations are more likely to be self-imposed. You will want to avoid elaborate plans which take time, money, and hard work and end up being left behind or unsuitable for another home. It's also unlikely that you will want a solid mahogany canopied bed for your child!

Your child does not need to live in a depressing, happenstance room because you rent or move frequently. If you view the problem in terms of the basic *impermanence* of the physical room, you will find innovative solutions. You are challenged to create an environment which is independent of the physical room itself. In other words, make a room which you can take with you. If you pay attention to *mobility* and *flexibility*, this will not be difficult.

Mobility is important because you will be hauling your child's room around with you. You will regret choices that are very heavy, bulky or superfluous. Give every item the test: is it worth carting around?

Flexibility is equally important. You need components that fit anywhere. Since rooms come in many shapes and sizes, furniture which is unusally long or odd-shaped is not practical. Consider furniture in terms of functional flexibility. If you are keeping your child's room to bare essentials, make sure each piece serves as many purposes as possible.

With these basic requirements in mind, here are a few ideas to help you create a successful and portable room for your child.

Furniture. Building block furniture is one option. If you select small mix and match modules, chests or boxes, you can treat each new room as a space to build blocks (or easily give the old room a new look). These blocks can be stacked and lined up to provide tables, chairs, headboards, storage, climbing structures, etc. When you move, simply fill them up and off you go. You have ready-made moving containers which fit in most cars.

105

Combining foam and plastic furniture is another option. You can used foam mattresses and lightweight plastic tables, chairs, and stacking modules. You might try inflatable furniture if you think it will last.

Free-standing structures solve all problems of impermanence by creating a room-within-a-room. A free-standing structure sits in the center of a room. It is a self-contained unit which includes sleeping, storage, work space, and activity areas. It should be designed to disassemble easily into portable sections. This solution may require expert help because of design complexities, but there are a few ready-made models available.

Walls. If you are fortunate enough to be in an older home with moldings, use them whenever possible. You can hang pictures, banners, even lightweight bookcases with special hooks that fit over the molding. No marks remain on the wall and whatever you hang can be changed easily.

Fabric cover-ups are easy and lightweight. If your child does not like the color of his walls and you can't paint them, make some large banners or buy a couple of attractive king-sized sheets. Small amounts of Velcro can be glued or stapled on walls and removed without damage. You can use these Velcro anchors to atttach the fabric, or glue the fabric to the walls with liquid starch. You can cover the entire wall or use one of the tent or canopy ideas discussed earlier. When you move, simply pull it down and take it with you. You can use the same piece of fabric in many different designs, and you can always put it on the bed.

White acrylic paper makes an excellent temporary wall covering. It can easily be pressed-on and peeled-off without leaving a residue on the wall and it comes in rolls. Your child can create his own walls with paint or crayons in the colors of his choice, or you can add a graphic. When you move or tire of the design, peel it off.

Color. Since you may have to accept the existing color of your child's room, it makes sense to keep all your major investments neutral. If the furniture is white, beige, brown or natural wood tones, it will fit anywhere. You may choose to keep rugs neutral-colored, as well, if you have a sizable investment in them. Use inexpensive accessories such as pillows, sheets, wastepaper baskets, simple curtains and the child's art work to supply color.

Windows and doors. The number and size of windows will vary from house to house, so it is best to keep window treatments easy and inexpensive. The most adaptable way to treat windows is to use gathered curtains on an adjustable spring rod. This rod, which is kept in place by pressure, doesn't leave marks or require hardware. It adjusts to varying lengths and can be placed at any height. When you move, just pop it out, take it to your new house, adjust it, and pop it back into the new window. This system works especially well with cafe curtains because full-length curtains may need to be lengthened or shortened. If you move frequently, curtains offer you more flexibility than shades, blinds, or shutters.

A flat topped hook made to fit over the top of a door will allow you to use some of the ideas for doors without marking the door at all. You can hang items like a bulletin board, chalk board, shoe bag, or storage sack from it.

Flooring. Flooring is a major investment that you cannot take with you. If you don't like your current floor, you can use a portable cover-up like a sturdy, neutral-covered area rug. It will provide warmth, comfort, and camouflage on a worn wooden floor. Likewise, it can cover worn or stained wall-to-wall carpeting or linoleum. Buy a rug or two that are small enough to fit most bedrooms and are easy to roll up and carry away.

These ideas are basic suggestions for creating a special place for your child which can go where he goes. Some of these ideas are illustrated in the following pages. You may even find them appealing for a permanent room. Because a portable room must respond to more limitations, it is often more innovative.

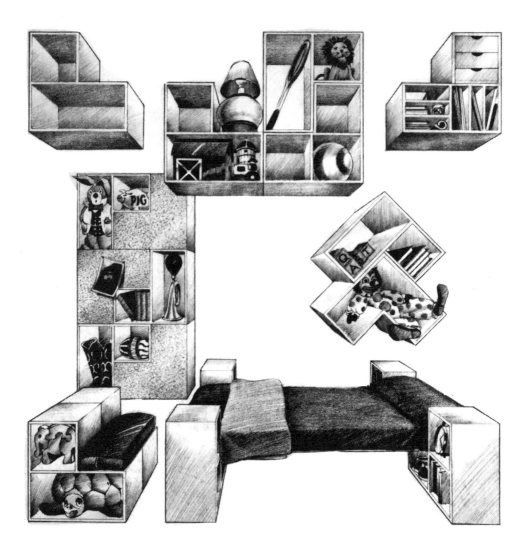

65. Here is an idea for an L-shaped module which has endless possibilities. You can make it yourself or have it made. The basic L can be stacked and placed to furnish storage, seating, bookcases, a two-sided divider, headboard, or sleeping pit, platform, climbing structure. Its spatial relationships are based on three cubes which you can make to fit your child's scale and specific requirements. For example, you may want them made to accommodate plastic dish bin drawers or certain sized shelving. The L requires one internal divider for stability, but you may want to add more for storage organization. They can even be stacked diagonally. Make them as sturdy and lightweight as possible and use them as moving containers.

66. *This design uses the thick slabs of polyurethane foam now available, covered with a washable fabric. Begin with a slab at least 12″ thick, long enough for a bed, and wider than needed for a bed. Make a wavy free-form line along one side to serve as a backrest. Foam suppliers will cut the foam for you with a special saw. When you put the smaller pieces on top of the larger piece, your child has a sofa. When put together on the floor, you have an amply wide bed. Turn the smaller piece wavy side up and you have created a contoured chair, or a dragon, or mountains, or ocean waves. The pieces are so lightweight that children can easily manage them. Make the covers removable for easy maintenance.*

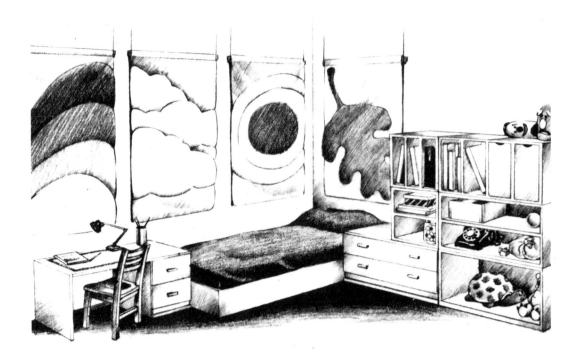

67. *This room consists of a group of small, easily portable units which can be stacked and placed in various arrangements. The desk surface is a plank supported by two storage units. The bed consists of a foam mattress on top of a 6" deep plywood platform. When you are ready to move, turn the bed platform over and fill it up. The banners are lightweight and colorful; they can be hung from molding or on walls with Velcro.*

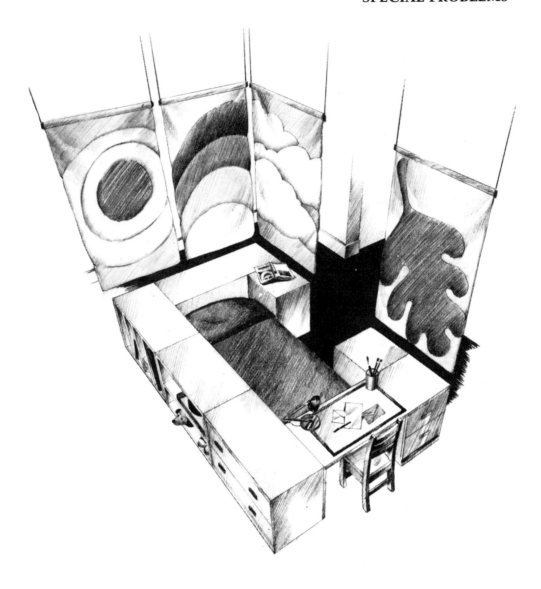

68. The same collection of furniture found in the preceding illustration can be rearranged to form a very different system in a new location. Here in a large room, everything is arranged in the center to provide a sleeping pit and work, play, and storage areas all in one self-contained system. The banners can be hung from the ceiling, creating a play "tunnel" behind them.

111

69. *This free-standing structure is a room-within-a-room which can be disassembled and set up anywhere. If you want to make one yourself, you may need some professional advice on stress, materials, and design. A few are available commercially. A free-standing structure should be very sturdy and safe. Beyond this, it should be easy to take apart and carry if you move frequently.*

4
Putting It All Together

By now you have made some basic decisions about what is feasible and desirable in your child's room. You may be ready to pull it together but feel uncertain about where to begin. Whether you have a room full of furniture that needs a design, or a plan in mind and an empty room, your first step is to buy some graph paper.

Making a Plan

You can save time and avoid costly mistakes if you draw your children's room to scale and try out your ideas on paper. You can make several plans and compare them visually. If your room plan is over-crowded or unbalanced, it will show up in your scale drawing. You can rectify it at this point without rearranging the furniture. Graphics and murals are easier to execute if they are tested in your scale drawing first. You can also try out color schemes before making any irrevocable decisions. Finally, when you want to purchase things, you will have all the necessary information in scale on one sheet of paper.

Maximizing floor space. As you are trying out various room arrangements on your scale drawing, give priority to those which maximize floor space. The importance of floor space in a child's room has already been discussed but it deserves special emphasis.

Floor space may not be crucial to an adult, but it is extremely important to a child. Children spend a great deal of their childhood

All dimensions shown in inches.

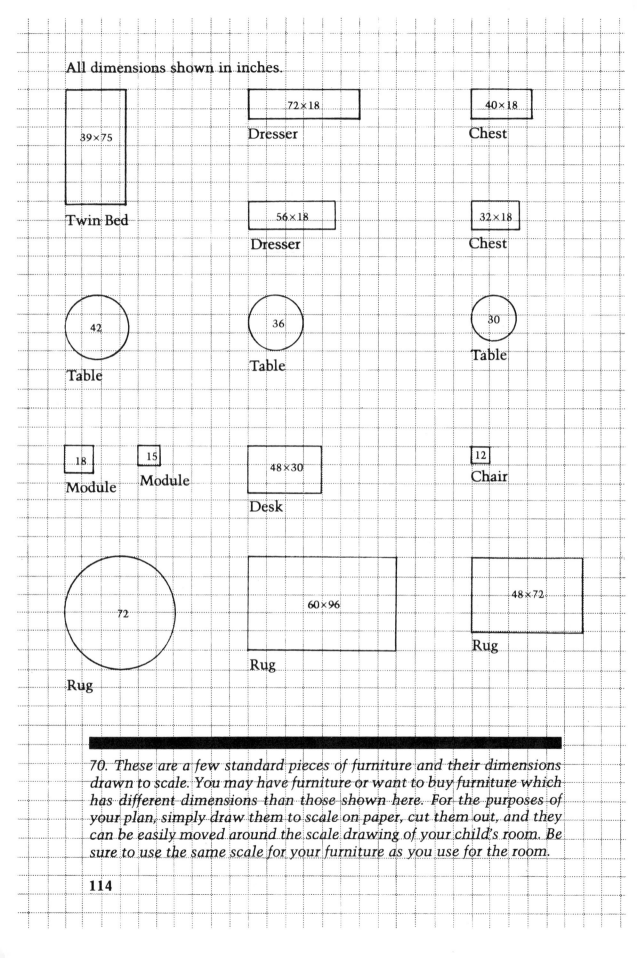

39×75

Twin Bed

72×18
Dresser

40×18
Chest

56×18
Dresser

32×18
Chest

42
Table

36
Table

30
Table

18
Module

15
Module

48×30
Desk

12
Chair

72
Rug

60×96
Rug

48×72
Rug

70. These are a few standard pieces of furniture and their dimensions drawn to scale. You may have furniture or want to buy furniture which has different dimensions than those shown here. For the purposes of your plan, simply draw them to scale on paper, cut them out, and they can be easily moved around the scale drawing of your child's room. Be sure to use the same scale for your furniture as you use for the room.

114

playing on the floor. Give them as much space as you can. They need room to romp and roll, set up trains, have a tea party, play monopoly, make a city out of blocks, ride their cars and rocking horses, run their trucks, spread out school projects, and so on. Review the list of space-saving ideas in the section on sharing a room.

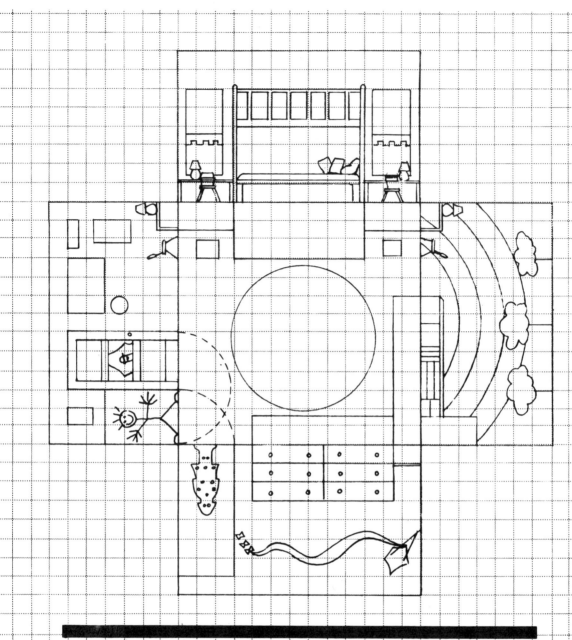

71. Make a scale drawing of your child's room by using five sheets of graph paper—one for the floor and four for the walls. The scale used here out of necessity is one square = one foot, but for convenience, you will probably want to use a larger scale. Carefully draw the room dimensions and add windows, doors, and any projecting beams. Use your paper furniture cut-outs to move around the floor drawing until you get an arrangement you like. Then, draw the walls as they would be viewed from the opposite wall. Everything will appear in only two dimensions, of course, but if you lay all five sheets together (as above), youcan get a reasonably accurate idea of how your child's room will appear. You can make copies of your final plan and try out different color schemes.

116

Convenience vs. appearance. Keep in mind the possible conflict between convenience and appearance as you finalize your plan. It's best to make convenience and comfort your first priority. Make it easy for your child to reach his closet, bed, desk and play area without encountering obstacles. Accommodate traffic patterns by encouraging direct routes to activity areas. Keep your child's furniture in scale with his height. Evaluate items like lamps with an eye for their safety and eliminate all potential fire hazards at this point in your plans.

Putting convenience and function first does not imply that the appearance of your child's room must suffer. It simply means that the room's appearance should *serve* his requirements, comfort, and convenience, not the other way around. Sometimes in the final stages of room planning, you are tempted to throw good sense to the wind because you find something irresistible. If you have a conflict between a favored decorating idea and your child's functional need, choose what's functional. If it does not serve your child's needs—both functional *and* aesthetic—grit your teeth and resist.

The pros and cons of themes. Many people like children's rooms organized around a particular theme. Magazines often feature rooms decorated to resemble a zoo, bunk house, garden, circus, ship, etc. Some of these rooms are enchanting and imaginative places. If your child spends his days zapping Darth Vader and wants his room turned into an inter-galactic spaceship, you may want to give him such a room. Before you run out for black paint and two thousand feet of aluminum foil, consider a few drawbacks of themes.

Theme rooms tend to be short-lived. Chances are, by the time you have spent a month of hard work and money transforming your child's room into a spaceship, he will have forgotten all about Darth Vader and have a new, all-consuming interest. The most delightful theme room becomes boring quickly if it's *over-defined*. It cannot be anything else but what you have made it.

Because of their detail, theme rooms can limit the growth and creativity of a child. A detailed theme room expresses the imagination of an *adult*, not the child who resides there. Such a room inhibits experimentation.

You can emphasize your child's current interests without turning his room into a theme room. You might provide your valiant spaceman with Darth Vader posters, Star Wars sheets, and a cardboard box spaceship. When he has moved on to afford to a new interest, you can change the sheets and posters. The cardboard box will now serve as a submarine, train, or race car.

You still might want to add a contribution of your own to your child's room. A tree, a mural, or a graphic can be an appealing addition to a child's room without limiting his own creativity. The point is not to *over-define* a room with a short-lived theme or invest in thematic accessories that you are not willing to change occasionally. Some of the most exciting children's rooms provide shapes and spaces which children can turn into anything they wish.

With these ideas, suggestions and guidelines, you can begin the challenging and creative process of designing your child's room. Don't let the possibilities overwhelm you: take one step at a time, list your priorities, and then have a wonderful time! When you know what you want, and are ready to start constructing, remember there are many sources to find out how to build, paint, sew, find deals, buy supplies, etc. etc. Look at books, talk to painters and carpenters, check around. The information is all around you, though you may have to spend some time seeking it out.

Designing, learning how, picking and choosing, and discovering what your child likes and wants can be a fulfilling creative and shared experience for everyone. Let your imagination be your guide, but most of all enjoy yourselves!